Athanasius and His Legacy

Athanasius and His Legacy

Thomas G. Weinandy and Daniel A. Keating

Fortress Press
Minneapolis

ATHANASIUS AND HIS LEGACY

Cover image: "Saint Athanasius," icon from Sozopol, Bulgaria, end of 17th century. Tempera on wood. Bulgarian national art gallery—Sofia.
https://commons.wikimedia.org/wiki/
File:Saint-Athanasius-of-Alexandria-icon-Sozopol-Bulgaria-17century.jpg

Cover design: Ivy Palmer Skrade

Print ISBN: 978-1-5064-0628-2

eBook ISBN: 978-1-5064-0629-9

The paper used in this publication meets the minimum requirements of American National Standard for Information Sciences — Permanence of Paper for Printed Library Materials, ANSI Z329.48-1984.

Manufactured in the U.S.A.

Dedicated to
John Henry Cardinal Newman

Contents

Preface xi

Part I. Athanasius's Trinitarian-Incarnational Soteriology

1. Athanasius and the Council of Nicaea *7*
2. The Trinity and the Holy Spirit *25*
3. Athanasius's Incarnational Soteriology *37*

Part II. The Contested Legacy of Athanasius

4. The Reception of Athanasius in the Eastern Tradition *55*
5. The Reception of Athanasius in the Western Tradition *73*
6. Contra and Pro Athanasius: Isaac Newton and John Henry Newman *87*
7. Contemporary Readings of Athanasius *105*

Bibliography *123*

Index of Names *129*

Preface

Within the Christian tradition, along with Basil the Great (ca. 329–79), Gregory of Nazianzus (329–ca. 389), and John Chrysostom (347–407), Athanasius (ca. 296–373) is recognized as one of the great fathers of the Eastern church. This brief study of Athanasius's thought and his reception throughout the centuries will, hopefully, demonstrate why such a designation is appropriate and even well deserved. This survey will also reveal that Athanasius was thought to be great not only because of his theological acumen but also because of his ardent defense of the full divinity of Jesus as the Son of God and his faithfulness to the Council of Nicaea. But herein lies the rub. While the ecclesial tradition hails Athanasius as a saintly theological defender of the faith, others, even in his own time, considered him a theological dogmatist and a partisan clerical thug. This interplay between "Athanasius the virtuous perceptive theologian" and "Athanasius the malevolent dogmatic zealot" will be a constant theme throughout our inquiry.

The first part of our study will examine Athanasius's theological thought. After providing a brief introductory biography of Athanasius, chapter 1 will examine his account, in keeping with the Council of Nicaea, of professing that the Son is truly God as the Father is God. Chapter 2 will investigate Athanasius's theology of the Trinity, particularly the divinity of the Holy Spirit. Chapter 3 will analyze Athanasius's theological understanding of the incarnation: the manner in which Jesus is the incarnate Son of God, being both fully divine and fully human. This first section was authored primarily by Thomas G. Weinandy.

The second part of our study will examine how Athanasius and his thought have been received over the centuries. Chapter 4 will assess how the Eastern Christian tradition received Athanasius and how his thought influenced them, focusing especially on Basil the Great, Gregory of Nazianzus, Cyril of Alexandria, and the monastic world. Chapter 5 investigates how the Western tradition received Athanasius, with a special concern for the West's reception of the "Athanasius Creed," a work that Athanasius did not compose. The contrasting reception of Athanasius's teaching and character by Isaac Newton and John Henry Newman respectively will occupy chapter 6. Lastly, chapter 7 will scrutinize contemporary theologians as to the lasting legacy of Athanasius's theological thought and the perennial debate over his enigmatic character. This second section was written primarily by Daniel A. Keating.

We hope that our brief monograph will stimulate further interest in Athanasius as a significant theologian even for our own day, as well as kindle curiosity in the fathers of the church as a whole. They lived in a different culture and intellectual milieu from our own, but they are, nonetheless, the original theologians within the Christian tradition and so still shape Christian belief today. We want to thank Professor Paul Rorem of Princeton Theological Seminary for inviting us to undertake this volume as part of the Fortress Press series Mapping the Tradition, and we are grateful to Michael Gibson, our editor, and the staff of Fortress Press for all of their help in shepherding this book through the publishing process.

Thomas G. Weinandy and Daniel A. Keating
Solemnity of the Annunciation, 2017

PART I

Athanasius's Trinitarian-Incarnational Soteriology

Introduction: A Brief Life of Athanasius

There is no definitive life of Saint Athanasius and many of the alleged events of his life are disputed. Nonetheless, to understand Athanasius's theology necessitates that we know, at least in summary, the doctrinal controversies of his time and how these debates affected him intellectually and personally. He did not live a tranquil life nor did he practice the art of theology within a serene environment.

Athanasius was born around 296 CE, though little can be ascertained for certain about his early life. During his youth both he and his mother were baptized, and Athanasius was subsequently educated by Alexander, the bishop of Alexandria. While studying contemporary philosophy and literature, his training, spiritually and intellectually, principally focused on the study and contemplation of Scripture. The defining event in Athanasius's life, one that he surely did not fully appreciate at the time, was attending, as a young deacon, the Council of Nicaea with Bishop Alexander. The Council of Nicaea (325), which defined the full divinity of the Son of God, would become Athanasius's cherished but incommodious friend who shadowed him throughout the course of his theological career and his ecclesial life. Nicaea would shape the whole of Athanasius's theology, and his defense of the Nicene doctrine would become the political catalyst for his later exiles. Without Nicaea, Athanasius would not have become the Athanasius we know—either fondly or disparagingly. As we will see in our study, his loyalty to Nicaea fashioned him, then and throughout history, into either a doctrinal champion in the view of some or an ecclesial reprobate in the view of others.

Alexander died three years after the Council of Nicaea, and Athanasius became the bishop of Alexandria on April 17, 328. Athanasius inherited a very complex ecclesial and social situation. Because of the leniency with which Athanasius's predecessors treated those who had lapsed during the Diocletian persecution in 313, Bishop Melitius of Lycopolis and his followers protested Athanasius's election, instigating a schism within the Egyptian church. Moreover, Alexandria was one of the most vibrant cities in the Roman Empire, being a major port and the agricultural capital of the empire. It boasted the world's largest library and was the academic home of the Stoics and Platonists. Not only did Egyptians inhabit this Roman-governed city, but also numerous Greeks, Jews, and other minority groups. Additionally, Alexandria was composed of pagan, Christian, Jewish, Gnostic, and Manichaean religious communities. This cosmopolitan mix of peoples, philosophies, and religions led to inevitable friction and even riots, everyone passionately competing for their rightful place within the polis. As the Christian bishop of Alexandria, Athanasius had to not only shepherd his own flock but also defend it within the chaotic civic life that was the Alexandria of his day.

Though Arius was condemned and exiled at the Council of Nicaea for denying the full divinity of Jesus, the emperor Constantine sought to bring him back. Bishop Alexander and, subsequently, Athanasius denied him full communion in the church. Many believe that it was at this time Athanasius wrote his first conjoined works, *Contra Gentes* and *De Incarnatione*, in which he expressed what he considered the true Gospel. Eusebius of Nicomedia, a sympathizer of Arius, and the Melitians renewed their attack on Athanasius, and, in response, Constantine called a council at Tyre. Composed mainly of Athanasius's opponents, the council condemned him, upheld Arius's theological position, and reinstated the Melitians. Athanasius appealed to Constantine, who was at first supportive. However, the emperor later exiled him to Gaul in 335, causing riots to break out in Egypt on Athanasius's behalf. After Constantine's death two years later, his three sons, who now governed the empire, allowed all exiled bishops to return to their respective dioceses. While Athanasius returned to cheering crowds, he was again soon under attack, resulting in a new bishop, Pistis, being elected in his place. Both Athanasius and Pope Julius protested the election because Pistis supported Arius. However, a new synod was held in Antioch, which installed another new bishop of Alexandria, Gregory, whose arrival in Alexandria caused riots even among the non-Christians. Athanasius fled to Rome at the invitation of Pope Julius. During this second exile, Athanasius wrote his major three-volume work, *Orationes contra Arianos* (339–43). This present study will focus, though not exclusively, on this work, for here Athanasius defends the divinity of Jesus as the Son of God by analyzing the disputed passages of Scripture.

Pope Julius called a synod in Rome hoping to reinstate Athanasius. However, this precipitated a whole series of counter synods that upheld an Arian or non-Nicene theological position and accused the Nicene Creed of being Sabellian—that is, sanctioning the view that the Father, Son, and Holy Spirit were merely various changeable expressions or modes of the one God and thus not truly "persons" in their own right. With the encouragement of Pope Julius, Emperor Constans held a council at Sardica in 343, which the Eastern "Arian" bishops refused to attend because of Athanasius's presence. The Western bishops, in turn, excommunicated the Eastern bishops. Emperor Constantius in the East and Emperor Constans in the West attempted to reconcile the various factions by holding a council in Antioch in 344; all of this had little effect. Constantius did, in the end, permit Athanasius to return to Alexandria in 346, thus ending his exile and initiating his longest residency in Alexandria—ten years.

Athanasius's return precipitated great jubilation among the populace of Alexandria. This joy was short lived, for Emperor Constans was assassinated by his general Magnetius, who later committed suicide when Emperor Constantius took up arms against him. Becoming the sole emperor, Constantius revived his anti-Nicene policies and so his opposition to Athanasius. Constantius called a number of councils, all of which condemned Nicaea's doctrine that Jesus, as the Son of God, was *homoousion* (consubstantial) with the Father. Athanasius vigorously responded by writing his *De Decretis* (ca. 352–53) in which he staunchly defended the *homoousion* doctrine and the validity of the Council of Nicaea. However, Constantius's tactics coerced many of the Western bishops to accept his pro-Arian doctrinal stance. Moreover, Constantius sent his secretary, Diogenes, to Alexandria to apprehend

Athanasius. Because of Athanasius's popular support, he was unsuccessful, but on February 8, 356, Diogenes, with the help of the Roman commander, launched a midnight raid on Athanasius and his congregation in the Church of Theonas. While Athanasius stealthily escaped with the help of his beloved monks and clergy, he now entered into his third exile (356–62).

While hiding among the desert monks, Athanasius wrote his *Apologia ad Constantium* and hoped to present it personally to the emperor. However, because Constantius also exiled all of the pro-Nicene Egyptian bishops as well as Pope Liberius, Athanasius abandoned his hope. The emperor deposed Athanasius and installed a new bishop who ruthlessly persecuted Athanasius's defenders. Once again, various councils where held in the hope of finding some resolution to the various theological positions concerning the Son's relationship to the Father. Bishop Basil of Ancyra proposed that the Son was *homoiousios* (of like nature) to the Father. However, the Western bishops, wanting to be loyal to Nicaea's *homoousion* doctrine, recognized that such a proposal was inadequate, for while the Son may be like in nature to the Father, this could mean that he was not truly God as the Father is God. Once again, Constantius attempted to force his pro-Arian doctrine upon all parties. In the midst of all this theological chaos and political nastiness, Athanasius, from his monastic desert hideout, was his most prolific. Besides his *Apologia ad Constantium*, he also authored his *Apologia de Fuga*, *Historia Arianorum ad Monacho*, and *De Synodis*. He also wrote his very influential *Vita Antonii* as well as his letters *Ad Serapionem*, in which he defends the divinity of the Holy Spirit, specifying that the Holy Spirit is also *homoousion* with the Father and the Son. Constantius died in 360 and his cousin Julian became emperor. The current bishop of Alexandria, George, had so angered the populace that a mob killed him. Julian, in 362, allowed all exiled bishops to return to their sees, and so Athanasius returned, but his stay would once again be fleeting.

Athanasius worked in this period to reconcile all the conflicting theological parties and various opinions. Those who held that the Son was *homoiousian* (of like nature) with the Father spoke of there being three *hypostases* within the Trinity. Those who upheld the Nicene *homoousion* doctrine preferred to speak of one *hypostasis*. At the Council of Alexandria (362), all parties agreed that one could speak of three *hypostases* (persons) as long as the oneness of God was maintained and that one could equally speak of one *hypostases* (nature) as long as one did not deny the authentic distinction between the Father, the Son, and the

Holy Spirit. Moreover, the council affirmed the full divinity of the Holy Spirit and that, within the incarnation, Jesus possessed not only a body but also a human soul or mind.

In the midst of these promising events, Emperor Julian, "the Apostate," rejected Christianity and attempted to restore paganism. Fearing Athanasius's theological and ecclesial standing, he stated that all bishops, while they could remain in their respective countries, could not govern their respective sees. He specifically said that Athanasius could not abide in Alexandria. This caused an outcry; Julian forced Athanasius to leave Egypt, resulting in his fourth exile. He resided again with his sympathetic desert monks and was able to return to Alexandria on the death of Julian in 363. Jovian, the new emperor, was friendly to Athanasius, but he died in 364 and was succeeded by Valentinian, who appointed his brother, Valens, as governor of the East. He opposed Nicaea and exiled all pro-Nicene bishops. Athanasius refused to leave and so Valens's general besieged the Church of Dionysios only to find that Athanasius had fled. Within months, because of the political and religious unrest in Alexandria due to Athanasius's absence, Valens allowed him to return.

Athanasius lived the remainder of his life in relative tranquility. Even when an anti-Nicene bishop came to Alexandria, so fervent were Athanasius's supporters that the bishop had to be ushered out of the city under military guard. During these years, Athanasius primarily concerned himself with christological issues, writing the letters *Ad Adelphium* and *Ad Epictetum*. Athanasius died on May 2, 373, having spent seventeen of his forty-six years as bishop in exile. He died assured that the Nicene Creed, for which he suffered and had spent his life espousing and defending, had prevailed.

1

Athanasius and the Council of Nicaea

"Athanasius against the world." Historically this was the epithet for Athanasius's singular defense and interpretation of the Council of Nicaea. As we saw in our brief biography, when almost all of the bishops, theologians, and emperors stood against him theologically, ecclesiastically, and politically, Athanasius resolutely endorsed and championed the Nicene Creed as a true expression of the Catholic faith. In this chapter, we will examine his doctrinal defense of the Son's true divinity and articulate his theological and scriptural arguments for why the Son is God as the Father is God. In the subsequent two chapters, we will also treat his defense and understanding of the Trinity, the divinity of the Holy Spirit, and the incarnation—all of which bear upon and are intertwined with Athanasius's refutation of Arius and various "Arian" formulas that subsequently emerged, as well as his proactive exposition of the Nicene Creed.[1]

1. For more complete studies of the thought of Athanasius see the following: Khaled Anatolios, *Athanasius: The Coherence of His Thought* (London: Routledge, 1998); Lewis Ayres, *Nicaea and Its Legacy: An Approach to Fourth-Century Trinitarian Theology* (Oxford: Oxford University Press, 2004); John Behr, *Formation of Christian Faith*, vol. 2, *The Nicene Faith*, 2 parts (Crestwood, NY: St. Vladimir's Seminary Press, 2004); David Brakke, *Athanasius and the Politics of Asceticism* (Oxford: Clarendon, 1995); George Dion Dragas, *St. Athanasius of Alexandria: Original Research and New Perspectives* (Rollinsford, NH: Orthodox Research Institute, 2005); James D. Ernest, *The Bible in Athanasius* (Leiden: Brill, 2004); Alvyn Pettersen, *Athanasius* (Ridgefield, CT: Morehouse, 1995); Thomas G. Weinandy, *Athanasius: A Theological Introduction* (Aldershot, UK: Ashgate, 2007); and Frances M. Young, *From Nicaea to Chalcedon: A Guide to the Literature and Background*, with Andrew Teal, 2nd ed. (Grand Rapids: Baker Academic, 2010).

The Making of the Crisis

To fully appreciate Athanasius's theology concerning the ontological relationship between the Father and the Son, we first need to provide a brief summary of the ever-growing theological crisis that preceded and precipitated the Council of Nicaea. From apostolic times, the church proclaimed that the Father, the Son, and the Holy Spirit were the one God of Abraham, Isaac, and Jacob. However, almost immediately, as one can imagine, the issue arose as to how God can be one yet all three "persons" truly be God. Many attempts were made to conceive properly and articulate clearly this mystery of faith—frequently in a flawed manner or in what would later be deemed a heretical manner. Paul of Samosata (third century CE), bishop of Antioch, proposed, in order to preserve the oneness of God, that Jesus was merely adopted as the Son of God at his baptism. Such a proposal, obviously, denied the divinity of the Son as well as the Holy Spirit. Sabellius (third century CE) and other modalists argued that the one God changed the manner or mode of his expression in keeping with revelation. In creating, for example, he expressed himself as Father; in the incarnation, he expressed himself as Son; and in sanctifying humankind, he changed his mode of expression to that of the Holy Spirit. In so doing, God remains the one God but expresses himself in three different manners. While Sabellius upheld the oneness of God and hoped to express how all the "persons" were divine, he sacrificed the substantial integrity of each of the divine subjects. The Father, the Son, and the Holy Spirit possessed no true ontological self-identity or depth.

Origen (ca. 185–ca. 254), following upon the apologists such as Justin Martyr (ca. 100–ca. 165), held that the Father possessed the fullness of the Godhead and from him, in a Platonic manner, the Son and the Holy Spirit eternally emanated. Importantly, for Origen, the Father was eternally the Father, for the Son eternally came forth from his very substance. Origen, then, believed he could uphold the oneness of God for the Son and Holy Spirit; while emanating out from him in a hierarchical manner, they each nonetheless shared in the Father's one divine nature. Moreover, the Son and Holy Spirit possessed their own subjective identity as persons (*hypostases*) distinct from the Father precisely because they emanated out from him. Thus, Origen believed that he could uphold the oneness of God as well as the distinction of persons. However, there is an irreconcilable tension within Origen's conception of the divine Triad. The Father alone possessed the fullness of the Godhead while the Son and Holy Spirit became lesser derivative expressions of it. The more the Son and Holy Spirit emanated out from the Father, and so attained their distinct identities, the less divine they became and also the less they were united with the Father—the Son being more divine than the Holy Spirit since the Holy Spirit emanated from the Father through the Son. Origen truly wanted to conceive and articulate the proper oneness and threeness within God, but he himself was aware of the tensions that resided within his attempt. Following Origen, theologians went in one of two directions. Some stressed the unity between the Father and the Son and so the full divinity of the Son; others emphasized the distinction between the Father and the Son and the Son's subordination to the Father, and therefore minimized his divinity. This seemingly irreconcilable tension, a tension that was percolating over several generations, gave rise to the crisis that would confront the Council of Nicaea and would fling Athanasius into the protracted theological, ecclesial, and political fray.

Here, we should note that two presuppositions gave rise to the above faulty conceptions, even when well-intended, concerning the issue of how God can be one while the Father, the Son, and the Holy Spirit can all be truly God. First, it has been presumed throughout, most noticeably in Origen, that the Father alone and singularly constituted the whole of the Godhead. This presupposition followed upon the Old Testament revelation where God revealed that he alone is the one God. This was reinforced within a Platonic and Aristotelian Greek philosophical milieu, where there is only one God as opposed to a plethora of deities. From within a Christian context this one God, whether biblical or philosophical, would be the Father. Similarly, Christian theologians, such as the apologists and Origen, could easily employ the Neoplatonic notion that all reality emanates out from God and so the Son and the Holy Spirit emanated out from the Father. However, as we will see, both presuppositions are false, and it will be the Council of Nicaea and Athanasius who will demonstrate their falsity. Athanasius will perceive that because of the revelation of Jesus as the Son of God and the sending forth of the Holy Spirit, the conceptualization of who the one God is needs to be radically reconceived—and this took place at the Council of Nicaea. However, Arius (d. 336), a priest of Alexandria, also took as a given these two presuppositions, but he did so knowing that within such preconditions it was impossible for God to be one and for the Son to be God. Here, we must briefly articulate why Arius was convinced that the Son was a creature.

Arius's Theological Position

Arius was not a systematic thinker and most of what we know about his theological stance is found within his opponents' rebuttals, primarily Bishop Alexander (d. 328) and Bishop Athanasius (ca. 296–373). We can, nonetheless, know the core of his arguments and conclusions. For Arius, God is transcendent in that he is not only other than all else, but also far removed from all else. He is ineffably one and there is none like him. Unlike creatures, God is defined as ingenerate or unoriginate, without beginning or end. Being alone ingenerate, God is alone unalterable and unchangeable. For Arius, since God alone is unchangeably ingenerate, it would be metaphysically impossible for him to generate another ingenerate being. Two ingenerate beings, one dependent upon the other, would be a contradiction of terms and would destroy the unique ingenerate oneness of God. For Arius, God is a "monad" in that he alone possesses a singular mode of existence. Moreover, Arius rightly perceived the flaw in the principle of emanation. If God is absolutely one and so alone constitutes the whole of the Godhead, it is impossible for him to share his divinity with another, for that would demand that he change and mutate into a multiplicity, thus destroying his immutable oneness. And so, if the Son came forth from the Father and so shared in his divine nature, this would demand that there be two Gods, dividing the one nature of God into two. Arius, in his seemingly impeccable logic, concludes that the Son must be a creature. If God is defined as ingenerate, then for the Son to be "begotten" must mean that he is not ingenerate, and if he is not ingenerate, then he must be generate, and if he is generate, he must be a creature. For Arius, if God is one, there is no possibility that the Son can be God. Because God is eternally ingenerate, Arius argued, he was not always the Father and only became Father when he created his Son, the first and most divine-like of all creatures. Athanasius sums up Arius's position:

> God was not always a Father: The Son was not always: But whereas all things were made out of nothing, the Son of God also was made out of nothing: And since all things are creatures, he also is a creature and a thing made: And since all things once were not, but were afterwards made, there was a time when the Word of God himself was not; and he was not before he was begotten, but he had a beginning of existence: For he has then originated when God has chosen to produce him: For he also is one among the rest of his works.[2]

In order to protect God's singular immutable transcendent nature, Arius held that, while the Father created the Son, the Son created all else that existed, thus becoming the protective shield between the transcendent God and all finite reality. Moreover, since the Son or Logos/Word is a creature, he possesses those attributes that accrue to finite reality such as being changeable. This is why the Son or Word could become flesh and equally why he could not be truly divine. In becoming human, the Son would undergo a change, and as a human being he could suffer and die. While a created spiritual being could endure such changes and limitations, God himself, because of his immutable transcendent singular existence, could not and so the incarnation equally demands that the Son be a creature, though he is the most divine-like of all that is created. Here, Arius employs a constellation of Scripture passages that appear to prove his point. The following is an example.

> How can the Son be from the Father by nature, and like him in *ousia*, who says, "All power is given unto me. . . ." If he was, as you [Nicenes] say, Son by nature, he had no need to receive but possessed it as a Son. Or how can he be the natural and true Power of the Father, who . . . says "Now is my soul troubled?" How can he be the Word of the Father, without whom the Father never was . . . who said upon the cross, "My God, my God, why hast thou forsaken me?" If the Son were, according to your interpretation, eternally existent with God, he would not have been ignorant of the [last] day, but would have known it as Word; nor would he have been forsaken who was coexistent; nor would he have asked to receive glory, who had it from the Father; nor would he have prayed at all; for being the Word, he needed nothing. But since he is a creature and one of the things originated, therefore he spoke in this way, and needed what he did not have, for it is proper to creatures to require and need what they do not possess.[3]

According to Athanasius, Arius and his followers "deny the Eternity and Godhead of the Word in consequence of those human attributes which the Saviour took on him by reason of that flesh he bore."[4]

Arius, then, denied the divinity of the Son on two fronts: the divinity of the Son necessitates a division and change in the one God that is metaphysically impossible, and the Son's becoming human

2. Athanasius, *Ad Episcopos Aegypti*, 12. All quotations from Athanasius are taken, unless otherwise noted, from *St. Athanasius: Select Works and Letters, Nicene and Post-Nicene Fathers*, series 2, vol. 4, trans. Philip Schaff and Henry Wace (T&T Clark: Edinburgh, 1986). The translation was primarily made by John Henry Cardinal Newman.
3. Athanasius, *Contra Arianos*, 3.26.
4. Ibid., 3.27.

necessitates that he not be God because the transcendent God cannot undergo change in becoming a human or the limitations and weaknesses that ensue upon his being human. Arius, thus, brought to a head the issue of how both God can be one and the Son can be God. Arius's position made it impossible to avoid this quandary and demonstrated that the flawed attempts to solve it would no longer serve. While the majority of the council fathers who gathered at Nicaea did not doubt that the one God is the Father and the Son and the Holy Spirit, they assembled unsure as to how they could adequately respond to Arius's seemingly flawless theological and philosophical logic.

The Council of Nicaea

By the imperial decree of Constantine, 318 bishops (traditionally reckoned) gathered at Nicaea in 325 CE. Previously, when questions of orthodoxy arose, bishops and synods would muster appropriate Scripture passages to refute an erroneous position. However, because Arius had raised the question of the Son's relationship to the Father to the ontological level, whether the Son was metaphysically God as the Father is God, Scripture passages could be interpreted in various ways. Those sympathetic to Arius's position were very disposed to affirm that the Son was "the only begotten Son of the Father," or "the perfect image of the Father." Because they had already determined that the Son was a creature, they could interpret such statements as meaning that the Son was the only creature created by/begotten of the Father, and thus, as the supreme creature, he is the perfect created image of the Father. The council was, therefore, required to make distinctions never before made, as well as to define the Son's divinity in a manner that would assure a proper reading and interpretation of Scripture. The result was the Creed of Nicaea:

> We believe in one God, the Father almighty, creator of all things, visible and invisible.
>
> And in our Lord, Jesus Christ, Son of God, the Only-Begotten from the Father, that is, from the substance [*ousia*] of the Father, God from God, light from light, true God from true God, begotten, not made, one in being/substance [*homoousion*] with the Father, through whom all things were made, those in heaven and those on earth,
>
> Who for us men and for our salvation came down and became flesh,

> was made man, suffered, and rose again on the third day, ascended into heaven and will come to judge the living and the dead,
>
> And in the Holy Spirit.
>
> However, those who say: "there was a time when he was not" and "before he was born he was not" and that he was made from nothing or who say that the Son of God may be of a different hypostasis or essence [*ousia*], or may be created subject to change and alteration, such persons the Catholic Church anathematizes.[5]

The council first declares that the one God is the Father and, in so doing, professes that the proper name of God is "Father" and not some philosophical concept such as Arius's "ingenerate." Biblical revelation holds exclusive pride of place. Moreover, since the eternal God is Father, so he must be eternally Father of the Son. There was never a "time/when" God was not the Father, and so there never was a "time/when" the Son was not. Likewise, the Father, being almighty, created all things and he did so by creating all things through his eternal Son. Thus, unlike Arius, God did not first create his Son, who then created everything else. The Father is transcendent in that he exists in a singular manner distinct from all else, but he does not exist such that he is infinitely removed from all else. The act of creation that ontologically distinguishes the Father from all else is the very same act that establishes his intimacy with all creation. That the Father creates all things through his Son/Word accentuates both the eternal divinity of the Son as well as distinguishes the Son from the Father and simultaneously highlights the communion of the Father and Son in that the Father through the Son together co-create.

The council next declared that as there is one Father, so there is "One Lord Jesus Christ" who is "the Son of God." Here, the council immediately tethers the divinity of the Son to the incarnation. Not only is the Son divine within the very being of God, but it is also the same divine Son who exists as a human being. This Son is "the Only-Begotten from the Father, that is, from the being/substance of the Father." As the only begotten Son, the Son is not ontologically a different kind of being from the Father, a creature, but he is begotten from the very same being or nature as the Father, that is, he is begotten as truly divine. If the Son were not begotten from the Father as truly divine,

5. Translation taken from Heinrich Denzinger, comp., *Compendium of Creeds, Definitions, and Declarations on Matters of Faith and Morals*, 43rd ed. (San Francisco: Ignatius Press, 2012), no. 125.

then the Father would not truly be the eternally divine Father, for he would not have an eternally divine Son whom he eternally begot. The Father is eternally constituted as "Father" in eternally begetting his Son. Because the Son is from the very being or substance of the Father, this begetting is "God from God, light from light, true God from true God." As one light enflames another light in which the first light is not diminished and the second light is distinct from the first, so God the Father begets God the Son, and so the Father and Son, while distinct, are both truly God.

Arius, as did many before him, held that to be "unoriginated" and "unbegotten" were synonymous, as were "originated" and "begotten." Thus, if the Father is unoriginated and so unbegotten, then the Son, if he is begotten must be originated and so must be a creature. Nicaea, for the first time, initiates an important clear distinction. Since the Son is from the substance/being of the Father and so truly God, the Son is "begotten, not made." What is begotten is always of the same nature as the begetter, and so the Son, as begotten, is of the same being/substance as the Father who begot him. God the Father created the world and so all creatures are of a different nature than God, but he begot his Son and so the Son shares in his very divine nature. Thus, while the Father is unbegotten and the Son is begotten, both are unoriginated in that the eternal Father eternally begets and does not make/create his eternal Son.

The council reaches its doctrinal climax in immediately proclaiming that the Son is *homoousion* (of one/same substance/being) with the Father. Since the Son is begotten of the substance of the Father—and so is true God and, therefore, begotten and not made—the Son is of the very same substance/being as the Father. While the council's use of this non-scriptural word would cause controversy, as we will see in Athanasius's defense of it, its insertion into the creed affirmed and confirmed that the Son is God in the same sense that the Father is God. It likewise, then, guaranteed that what was proclaimed in the New Testament concerning the Son's divinity be interpreted metaphysically, that is, for the Son to be "the only begotten" from the Father and so the perfect image of the Father was for him to be ontologically God as is the Father.

One of the issues that would confront Athanasius, especially in his defense of the council's use of the concept and term, was how *homoousion* should be understood and interpreted. Part of the difficulty was that *homoousion* could be understood in two problematic senses. First, it could be interpreted to mean that the Father and the Son were *homoousion* in that they generically shared the same substance, similar to two copper coins being *homoousion* because they shared the same substance of copper. If one understood *homoousion* in this sense, while the Father and Son would both equally be God, they would be two Gods just as there are two copper coins. Such an understanding would confirm Arius's claim that there is no way that one can simultaneously uphold the oneness of God and the full divinity of the Son. Historically, this would not seem to be the understanding of the Nicene fathers. They were rarely accused of asserting two equal divinities.

Second, *homoousion* could have been understood to mean that the Father and the Son were one and the same substance in that they were one and the same being or entity. While some scholars think this second understanding was highly unlikely among the fathers, it is precisely this interpretation, as we will see, that causes the future critics of Nicaea to accuse it of heresy. If one was an Origenist bishop, especially with Arian sympathies, who held that the Father constituted the whole of the Godhead, and then were faced with Nicaea's declaration that the Father and the Son were of the same one substance, one could easily conclude that the Father and the Son possess the same personal identity. This would be a form of Sabellian modalism. Such an understanding would cause, as Athanasius knew well, interminable debates, leading some to propose that the Son should be said to be *homoiousian* (of like being/substance) with the Father, so as to preserve the distinction between the Father and the Son.

While it is impossible to know with any accuracy which of the two understandings of *homoousion* the individual fathers at Nicaea held, if either of them, what can be said for certain is that they did wish to affirm the Son's full divinity with the Father and, as clearly implied within the Creed, the distinct and individual identities proper to the Father and the Son. Thus, Nicaea wanted both to uphold simultaneously the ontological integrity of the Father and the Son as well as their being the one God, the same metaphysical entity or being. In the prolonged course of his interpretation and defense of the Nicene Creed, Athanasius would be forced not only to censure Arius's and his followers' errors but also to articulate and so clarify Nicaea's doctrinal affirmations.

While it does not pertain to the Son's full divinity with the Father, which is the topic of this chapter, the council declared that the Son who is truly God, *homoousion* with the Father, is the same Son "who for us men and for our salvation came down and became flesh, was made man, suffered, and rose again on the third day, and will come to judge the living and the dead." This incarnational proclamation, as we will see, will be very important when it comes to Athanasius's own future defense and understanding of the incarnation. Likewise, it provides the basis for Athanasius's soteriological, Trinitarian, and christological thought. Only if Jesus is truly the divine Son of God who actually became an authentic human being could humankind be saved.

Lastly, Nicaea makes an ever so slight reference to belief in the Holy Spirit. Toward the end of the Arian conflict, Athanasius will be, nonetheless, one of the first to provide a biblical and theological justification for and vindication of the Holy Spirit's full divinity with the Father and the Son—even stating that the Holy Spirit, in keeping with Nicaea's doctrinal program, is *homoousion* with the Father and the Son.

Having briefly examined the theological milieu prior to Arius, the crisis that Arius precipitated, and the Council of Nicaea, which attempted to terminate the crisis and so bring doctrinal peace, we will now examine Athanasius's passionate championing and zealous elucidation of the Nicene doctrine, for the council did not bring concord but prompted a chaotic and protracted theological, ecclesial, and political conflict.

Athanasius's Refutation of the Arians and his Articulation of the Nicene Doctrine

Before delving into Athanasius's theological conception of how God can be one while simultaneously upholding the full divinity of the Father and the Son, a few preliminary remarks are necessary. First, while scholars debate whether Athanasius wrote his twofold work, *Contra Gentes* and *De Incarnatione*, before or soon after the Council of Nicaea, both works demonstrate that his ensuing compositions did not arise out of a theological vacuum. They argue for the full divinity of the Son/Word in relationship to the Father and that together they are the one God. Secondly, Athanasius articulated his early position from within the conjoining relationship of Scripture and tradition, that is, the living apostolic faith of the church is but the doctrinal expression of what is proclaimed in Scripture. He will continue to employ this Scripture-tradition alliance within all of his subsequent writings. Third, soteriology lies at the heart of Christian doctrine. Throughout Athanasius's entire corpus, beginning with his initial twofold work, upholding the full divinity of the Son/Word in relationship to the Father, and so the oneness of God, is essential for humankind's salvation, for only if the man Jesus is truly the divine Son of God is redemption assured. For Athanasius, as we will see, the doctrines of the Trinity and the incarnation are inherently soteriological, and the whole of his soteriological theology is founded upon these two doctrinal truths.

Unsurprisingly then, Athanasius structures his early major three-volume work, *Contra Arianos*, around the disputed Scriptures surrounding the divinity of the Son. (We will especially see this when examining Athanasius's understanding of the incarnation.)

> For, behold, we take divine Scripture . . . and set it up as a light upon its candlestick, saying:—Very Son of the Father, natural and genuine, proper to his essence, Wisdom, Only begotten, and very and only Word of God is he; not a creature or work, but an offspring proper to the Father's essence. Wherefore he is very God, existing one in essence with the very Father.[6]

For Athanasius, the Scriptures themselves proclaim that "our Savior," "our Lord Jesus Christ," is "God and Son of the Father."[7] Only if the man Jesus is the true divine Son of the Father could he in truth proclaim: "He who sees me has seen the Father" (John 14:9), "because the Son's essence is proper to the Father, and he in all points like the Father."[8] Only to Jesus, and not to angels, did "the Father show him to be his own proper and only Son, saying, 'You are my Son,' and 'This is my beloved Son, in whom I am well pleased.'"[9]

For Athanasius, then, unlike Arius, God is primarily defined by the biblical term "Father" and not by the philosophical designation "unoriginated." Moreover, for God to be the eternal Father demands that he is eternally the Father of the Son. "Since the Father is always, so is the Word," for "how can he speak truth concerning the Father, who denies the Son."[10] For God to be Father necessitates that he is Father of the Son. Therefore, being inseparable from his Father, "never was there when he (the Son) was not, but he was always; and being the Father's Image and Radiance, he has the Father's eternity."[11] There

6. Athanasius, *Contra Arianos*, 1.9.
7. Ibid., 1.10.
8. Ibid., 2.22.
9. Ibid., 2.23.
10. Ibid., 2.56 and 1.18; see also 1.11–12, 1.21, and 2.41. See also Athanasius, *De Decretis*, 12. In many of these passages, Athanasius quotes multiple Scriptures demonstrating that the Father and the Son/Word share the same divine attributes: eternity, everlasting power, wisdom, truth, shepherd, king, and so on, and above all the divine name, I AM.
11. Athanasius, *Contra Arianos*, 3.28; see also 2.57.

is an inherent ontological, relational bond between the Father and the Son, and so "when we call God Father, at once with the Father we signify the Son's existence."[12]

Athanasius also makes a very important biblical distinction, one that is relevant today. While "unoriginate" defines God in relationship to the created order (that which is originated), it does not essentially define God in himself. "And as the word 'Unoriginate' is specified relatively to the things originated, so the word 'Father' is indicative of the Son. And he who names God Maker and Framer and Unoriginate, regards and apprehends things created and made; and he who calls God Father, thereby conceives and contemplates the Son."[13] God, therefore, has revealed himself to be, in his very essence, Father of his Son. To designate the Son as "originate," and so a creature, not only dishonors him but also dishonors the Father, for the Father then is constituted "Father" only in relation to his created Son and not Father in his very divine being, that is, the eternal Father of the Son. "Therefore it is more pious and truthful to signify God from the Son and call him Father, than to name him solely from his works and call him Unoriginate. . . . [For] the title Father has its significance and bearing only from his Son."[14] Athanasius emphasizes that Jesus himself, as Son, taught his followers not to pray to "God Unoriginate" but to "Our Father." Likewise, Jesus commanded the church to baptize "not in the name of the Unoriginate and Originate, nor into the name of the Uncreated and the Created, but into the name of the Father, Son and Holy Spirit, for with such an initiation we too are truly sons; and using the name Father, acknowledge from that name the Word in the Father."[15] Here, we perceive Athanasius's soteriological emphasis. The whole point of the divine Son becoming one of us was to make "us sons of the Father, and deify men by becoming himself man."[16] Thus, human beings are able to be assumed, through baptism, into the intimate divine life of the Trinity as Spirit-filled children of the Father only if the one who assumed humankind's flesh is indeed the Father's fully divine Son. Thus, for Athanasius, the perfection of the Father's eternal fatherhood resides precisely in his eternally begetting his Son, whose eternal perfection lies precisely in his being the exact image of his Father. Humankind's salvation, for Athanasius, is predicated upon the

12. Ibid., 3.6.
13. Ibid., 1.33.
14. Ibid., 1.34.
15. Athanasius, *De Decretis*, 31.
16. Athanasius, *Contra Arianos*, 1.38; see also 1.39–40.

perfect and inseparable divinity of the Father and the Son, for it is into that perfect and inseparable divine unity that saved humanity comes to share.

Following upon Nicaea's distinction, Athanasius insists that "begetting" and "making" are entirely different notions. While God is unoriginate, this does not necessitate that the Son be a creature. The Arians "must constantly be told that the Son as well as the Father must . . . be called unoriginated," in that both existed eternally. Moreover, for the Father to be "unbegotten" and for the Son to be "begotten" does not mean that the Father "made" (originated) his Son as he did creatures, but rather that the Father eternally "begot" his Son and so the Son, as begotten, is the same nature as the Father who begot him.[17] Athanasius is clear that what is made is of a different nature than the maker. What is begotten is always of the same nature as the begetter. God made the world, but he begot his Son. One must remember, however, that unlike creaturely begetting where the begotten becomes a distinct, separate entity from the begetter, within the one God, while the Father and Son possess distinct identities, they are not separate beings.

Ensuing upon this, Athanasius stresses throughout *Contra Arianos* that the Son is begotten from the same *ousia* (nature) of the Father. While creatures possess a different nature than the Father and so are distinct beings, the Son, as the Father's Word and Wisdom, is not external to the Father but "is ever the proper offspring of the Father's *ousia* [nature]."[18] To be the "proper offspring" means that the Son is "not foreign but proper to the Father's *ousia*."[19] For Athanasius, for the Son to be begotten of the Father demands that he shares the Father's same divine nature, "for it is all one to say that God is wholly participated," and therefore the Son "has the real and true identity of nature with the Father."[20] To grasp the true meaning of Nicaea's proclamation that the "Only-Begotten" is "from the same substance of the Father" is to perceive that the Son shares equally the Father's very divine nature.

Without referencing Nicaea's *homoousion* at this point, Athanasius grasps that the council, in professing the Son's full divinity, declared the ontological participatory nature of the one God. Commenting on John 14:11, Athanasius writes:

17. See ibid., 1.31–32 and 2.4–5.
18. Athanasius, *Contra Arianos*, 1.29; see also 2.22, 24, 57, 82; 3.16–17, 63.
19. Ibid., 2.32; see also 3.19.
20. Ibid., 3.22 and 1.16.

> For the Son is in the Father . . . because the whole being of the Son is proper to the Father's *ousia*, as radiance from light and a stream from a fountain; so that whoso sees the Son, sees what is proper to the Father and knows that the Son's being, because from the Father, is the Father and is therefore in the Father. For the Father is in the Son, since the Son is what is from the Father and proper to him, as there is in the radiance the sun, and in the word the thought, and in the stream the fountain: for whoso thus contemplates the Son, contemplates what is proper to the Father's *ousia*, and knows that the Father is in the Son.[21]

Because the Father and the Son co-inhere in one another, they together express "the identity of the Godhead and the unity of *ousia*."[22] "The fullness of the Father's Godhead is the being of the Son, and the Son is the whole of God."[23] The Son "is proper to the Father's *ousia* and one in nature with it."[24] For Athanasius, Christian worship bears witness to this truth. "He who worships and honors the Son, in the Son worships and honors the Father, for the Godhead is one."[25] Moreover, because the Father and the Son are one and the same God, both equally share the same divine attributes. The Son is "Almighty," "Lord," "Light," "Forgiver of Sins," for "the Son is the Father's All."[26]

Even within this early refutation of Arianism and exposition of the Nicene doctrine, Athanasius argues that the Father and the Son are not distinct and separate natures but one and the same *ousia*. Thus, Athanasius does not suggest that the Father and Son share the same *ousia* in the generic sense, as two copper coins share the same *ousia*, but that they are one and the same entity or being, one and the same God. Likewise, while the Father and the Son are one and the same God, they possess their own distinct identities. It is the Father who begets his Son and so shares with him his very nature, and the Son is begotten of the Father and so properly shares in the Father's very nature. The one God is the Father begetting his Son, and so the Father's divine being belongs properly to the Son and the Son's divine being is properly from the Father.

It has often been remarked that prior to 350—that is, twenty-five years after the Council of Nicaea—Athanasius in his three volume *Contra Arianos* only once made reference to the Nicene *homoousion*. There,

21. Ibid., 3.3; see also 2.35 and 3.59.
22. Athanasius, *Contra Arianos*, 3.4; see also 3.20.
23. Ibid., 3.6.
24. Ibid., 1.58; see also 2.41.
25. Ibid., 3.6; see also 2.23.
26. Ibid., 3.67; see also 2.18.

he stated that the Son "is very God, existing *homoousion* with the very Father."[27] While Athanasius did state, as we already quoted, that the Son "is proper to the Father's *ousia* and one in nature with it," the question arises as to why he did not employ the term *homoousion* more often in his defense and articulation of the Son's full divinity. There is no obvious reason, but one could suggest that Athanasius decided to make his point primarily and almost solely from within a biblical perspective, that is, upon the ontological relationship that exists within the proper understanding of God the Father being the Father of his divine Son. This would demand that the Son, as the proper begotten offspring of the Father, share in his one divine nature. For Athanasius, the biblical testimony was in itself adequate for articulating and defending both the oneness of God and the authentic divinity of the Father's Son. However, as the theological, ecclesial, and political conflict intensified and the denunciation of Nicaea became more unyielding, Athanasius probably perceived that a biblical defense was no longer sufficient. The muddled situation propelled him to come to the defense of the Nicene *homoousion* and in so doing clarify its meaning.

The critics of Nicaea indicted its use of *homoousion* on four counts: (1) it was not a biblical term, (2) the Council of Antioch (268 CE) condemned it, (3) it either demanded that there be two Gods, or (4) it espoused a variety of Sabellianism. The more Athanasius addressed these concerns within the ensuing impassioned dispute, the more he became aware that *homoousion* was critical for upholding the biblical Nicene doctrine and, thus, for sustaining his own biblical defense and articulation of the Son's full divinity with his Father. For Athanasius, only the term *homoousion* authenticated and guaranteed the proper reading of Scripture.

In his justification of Nicaea's use of a non-scriptural word, Athanasius ironically points out that the Arians themselves employed non-scriptural words such as "ungenerate" and "there was a time when he was not." Athanasius argues that it is precisely because Arius and his sympathizers perfidiously misrepresented the Scriptures, giving to such terms and phrases as "only-begotten," "like," and "image" their own deceitful meaning, that the council fathers "were compelled on their part to collect the sense of Scripture, and re-say and re-write what they had said before, more distinctly still, namely that the Son is '*homoousios*' with the Father."[28] For Athanasius, even if Nicaea uses

27. Ibid., 1.9.

non-scriptural language, it does so precisely to guarantee and validate the proper reading of the sacred text, for "they contain the sense of the Scriptures, and expressing it, they convey it to those who have their hearing unimpaired for religious doctrine."[29] Athanasius's apology for Nicaea's use of a non-scriptural word and concept is still valid today, for its *homoousion* doctrine continues to guard against erroneous biblical readings and interpretations of who Jesus is as the Father's Son.

In addressing the other allegations against the council's usage of *homoousion*, Athanasius both exposes their inherent fallacies as well as clarifies a proper understanding of the council's intent. Athanasius acknowledges that the Council of Antioch had condemned the use of the term *homoousion*, but he immediately demonstrates that it condemned a false use of it. In censuring Paul of Samosata, the council understood the term in a materialistic sense, and so, if the Son was *homoousion* with the Father, this would demand that God be divided into two Gods—similar to two copper coins being *homoousion*. The fathers of Antioch "said with good reason, that Christ was not *homoousios*." The Council of Nicaea, however, professed a very different understanding. This council did not employ it in a materialistic sense but recognized that the Son was of the Father's very nature, and because of this, he was "not of a different nature, as we are, and not separate from the Father, but that, being from him, he exists indivisible, as radiance is with respect to light."[30] *Homoousion* must now be understood as expressing the full divinity of the Son and the oneness of God, for he and the Father share one and the same *ousia*. Thus, for Athanasius, the accusation that the council professes two Gods is false, for the Father's begetting of his Son is eternally constitutive of God's one nature. The one God is the Father begetting the Son, and so the Son is *homoousion* with the Father, for together they share one and the same divine *ousia*.[31] The "begetting" is not an act that takes place outside the being of God, or an act that causes alteration, change, or division within God. The "begetting" is the unalterable act by which the Father is eternally the Father of his Son. Thus, unlike all of Athanasius's theological predecessors, such as Origen, the Father does not singularly constitute the whole of the Godhead. Rather, his very name demands

28. Athanasius, *De Decretis*, 20. See also ibid., 18; Athanasius, *Ad Afros Epistola Synodica*, 5–6; and Athanasius, *Ad Episcopos Aegypti*, 1–4.
29. Athanasius, *De Decretis*, 21. See also Athanasius, *De Synodis*, 39.
30. Athanasius, *De Synodis*, 45.
31. See Athanasius, *Contra Arianos*, 1.15, 16, 21, 28; Athanasius, *Ad Episcopos Aegypti*, 16; Athanasius, *De Synodis*, 41, 51; and Athanasius, *De Decretis*, 24.

that he be the Father of his Son, and, equally, the Son must then be the Son of the Father. Thus, the Son is *homoousion*, one in being, with the Father.

The most challenging accusation against Nicaea was that of Sabellianism. As noted when examining the Nicene Creed, if one continued to hold, as did the later Origenist bishops, that the Father alone constituted the whole of the Godhead, then to say that the Son was *homoousion* with the Father could easily be interpreted to mean that the Son and the Father are identical. However, Athanasius assures these critics that "the Father is ever the Father and never could become the Son, so the Son is ever Son and never could become the Father."[32] Even though Jesus stated that he and the Father are one and that the Father is in him and he is in the Father (see John 10:30 and 14:10) and so manifests that they are one *ousia*, for Athanasius, they are not "one thing twice named, so that the same becomes at one time Father, at another his own Son, for Sabellius, holding this, was judged a heretic. But they are two, because the Father is Father and is not the Son, and the Son is Son and not the Father—but the nature is one."[33] In designating himself as Son and the Father as Father, Jesus manifests that while they are the one God, they are distinct in their unique identities. Athanasius states that Nicaea, in employing the term *homoousion*, adamantly upholds this truth.

> Neither do we hold a Son-Father, as do the Sabellians, and call him *monoousion* but not *homoousion* and thus destroying the existence of the Son. . . . For neither is the Father the Son, nor the Son the Father. For the Father is the Father of the Son, and the Son, Son of the Father.[34]

The Father and the Son are not identical as to *who* they are and so are not *monoousian* (one and the same subject), but they are identical as to *what* they are (one and the same God), and as such the Son is *homoousion* with the Father. Thus, for Athanasius, the Nicene *homoousion* doctrine clearly articulates and resolutely confirms both the distinction of the Father and the Son as well as their oneness as God.

Nonetheless, as the unrelenting dispute careened from one theological option to another, some advocated the term *homoiousios*, like in substance. They did so to ensure the proper integrity of the Father and the Son. Basil of Ancyra proposed such a position and wanted to speak

32. Athanasius, *Contra Arianos*, 1.22.
33. Ibid., 3.4.
34. Athanasius, *Expositio Fidei*, 2.

of the Son being "from the *ousia*" of the Father. Athanasius admired such efforts, but observed that *homoiousian* does not necessarily mean that the Father and the Son were "of the same *ousia*" and so equally divine.[35] Athanasius perceived that *homoiousian* allowed the Arian party to agree that the Son is of like substance to the Father but not the same substance as the Father, and so not ontologically God. Only *homoousion* ensured that the Son of God is ontologically God as the Father is God.[36]

> [Because the Son is] the genuine offspring of the Father's *ousia*, it would follow that he is inseparable from the Father, being connatural, because he is begotten from him. And this being the case, for good reason should he be called *homoousion*. . . . [For] the Son, being an offspring from the *ousia*, is one by *ousia*—himself and the Father who begat him.[37]

Conclusion

It may appear that throughout the strident debate and ecclesial and political intrigues, the simple faith of the gospel was lost amid elusive theological and philosophical subtleties. During the later debate over which term was more apt, *homoousion* or *homoiousian*, the exasperated cry was heard: "What difference does an iota make?" Yet, Athanasius rightly perceived that it was the simple gospel that he was defending and that the salvation of the world demanded the erasure of that little "iota." Only if Jesus was truly the divine Son, *homoousion* with the Father, was salvation assured. Moreover, Athanasius also was convinced that the mystery of the Trinity was clarified and preserved, and not dissolved, in the acid of philosophical rationalism.

As the Nicene doctrine was finally winning the field, a new theological issue concerning the Trinity arose: Was the Holy Spirit truly divine? If so, what distinguished the Holy Spirit from the Son? Athanasius, as one can imagine, eagerly and promptly jumped into this discussion. He did so, again, from within his own previously articulated biblical theology of the Trinity and of the Holy Spirit's place within it. It is to this issue that we now turn.

35. Athanasius, *De Synodis*, 41.
36. See ibid., 53–54.
37. Ibid., 48.

2

The Trinity and the Holy Spirit

In the preceding chapter, we examined Athanasius's defense and exposition of the Creed of the Council of Nicaea. We specifically focused on his theological account of the ontological relationship between the Father and the Son, demonstrating that, for Athanasius, they are equally God and that together they constitute the one nature of God—the Father eternally begetting his Son. While he did not discuss at length in his anti-Arian/pro-Nicene works his understanding of the Trinity or, specifically, the divine status and role of the Holy Spirit, neither topic is completely absent from his mind. In this chapter, we will survey Athanasius's understanding of the Trinity within his anti-Arian tracts, and then turn to his later work, that is, his *Letters to Serapion*. While Basil the Great is often credited with writing the first treatise specifically on the Holy Spirit, it is Athanasius, in his *Letters*, who actually provides the first extensive defense of and theological treatment on the full divinity of the Holy Spirit, and he does so in a manner that is more scripturally robust and theologically mature than the later Basil. With this in mind, we will first discuss how Athanasius conceives the Trinity.

Trinitarian Doxology and the Sacrament of Baptism

Within his critique of the Arian position and his championing of the Nicene doctrine, Athanasius consistently speaks of the Trinity within a doxological context: "To the God and Father is due the glory, honor and worship, with his co-existent Son and Word, together with the All-holy and Life-giving Spirit, now and to the endless ages of ages. Amen."[1] Athanasius insists that he does not worship the Son/Word as creature, but rather he worships the one God who "created all things through his Word, the only-begotten Son our Lord Jesus Christ, through whom to thee Father, together with the same Word, in the Holy Spirit, be glory and power forever and ever. Amen."[2] The Arians held that, since there is eternally only one God, it was only "when" God created the Son and the Holy Spirit that he became Father. "But this is not so; perish the thought; the Triad is not originated, but there is an eternal and single Godhead in the Triad, and there is one glory of the Holy Triad." For Athanasius, "the faith of Christians acknowledges the blessed Triad as unalterable and perfect and ever what is was, never adding to it what is more, nor imputing to it any loss . . . and therefore dissociates it from things generated, and guards as indivisible and worships the unity of the Godhead itself."[3]

From within this Trinitarian doxological setting Athanasius perceives the divinity of the Holy Spirit. As the term *Father* implies the term *Son* and thus their communion within the one nature of God, so the Holy Spirit cannot be "parted from him that sent him [Father], or from him who conveyed him [Son]."[4] For Athanasius, since the fathers at the Council of Nicaea spoke of the Son being *homoousion* with the Father, they did not "make the Holy Spirit alien from the Father and the Son, but rather glorified him together with the Father and the Son, the one faith of the Holy Triad, because there is in the Holy Triad also one Godhead."[5]

By placing the Holy Triad within a doxological milieu, Athanasius is able to confirm a number of Trinitarian truths. Since the Father, the Son, and the Holy Spirit are all equally worshiped, one must conclude that they are all equally divine, otherwise Christians would be performing idolatrous acts. Being all divine, one must also conclude that

1. Athanasius, *De Decretis*, 32.
2. Athanasius, *Historia Arianorum*, 80. See also Athanasius, *Apologia de Fuga*, 27.
3. Athanasius, *Contra Arianos*, 1.18.
4. Athanasius, *De Sententia Dionysii*, 17.
5. Athanasius, "To the Emperor Jovian," 4. See also Athanasius, *Contra Arianos*, 3.15.

the Father, the Son, and the Holy Spirit are all eternal and, as such, unoriginated, perfect, and unchangeable. Importantly, since the act of worship distinguishes the Father, the Son, and the Holy Spirit, they must possess their own unique and unconfused identities. Lastly, the very same act of worship nonetheless demands that the Father, the Son, and the Holy Spirit are all equally the one God, for it is the one Triadic God that Christians worship. Thus, Christian doxological prayer bears witness to the divine eternal unity of the Father, the Son, and the Holy Spirit as the one unchanging perfect God.

The divine Triad, for Athanasius, is not simply worshiped for its own sake but is also imperative for human salvation. This is seen within his theology of baptism, for one is baptized in the name of the Father, the Son, and the Holy Spirit and so taken up into their divine communion. The Son eternally possesses the Spirit of his Father and when he became flesh, the Father said: "Receive the Holy Spirit." "When he [Jesus] is baptized, it is we who are baptized in him. . . . He sanctifies himself, that we might be sanctified in him."[6] Commenting on 1 John 4:14, Athanasius states:

> For the Son does not merely partake of the Spirit, that therefore he too may be in the Father, nor does he receive the Spirit, but rather he supplies it himself to all; and the Spirit does not unite the Word to the Father, but rather the Spirit receives from the Word . . . and by participation of the Spirit we are knit into the Godhead; so that our being in the Father is not ours, but is the Spirit's which is in us and abides in us. . . . [Thus] the Son is in the Father in one way, and we become in him in another way, and that neither we shall ever be as he, nor is the Word as we. . . . For he . . . gives the Spirit, and whatever the Spirit has, he has from the Word. . . . For since the Word is in the Father, and the Spirit is given from the Word, he wills that we should receive the Spirit, that, when we receive it, thus having the Spirit of the Word which is in the Father, we too may be found on account of the Spirit to become one in the Word, and through him in the Father. . . . For what the Word has by nature, as I said, in the Father, that he wishes to be given to us through the Spirit irrevocably. . . . And so we are sons and gods because of the Word in us, so we shall be in the Son and in the Father, and we shall be accounted to have become one in the Son and in the Father, because that Spirit is in us, which is in the Word which is in the Father.[7]

In this rather convoluted passage, Athanasius is articulating how

6. Athanasius, *Contra Arianos*, 1.48.
7. Ibid., 3.24–25.

human beings, through baptism, come to participate in the life of the divine Triad. He does this by differentiating the manner in which the Son and Holy Spirit are related to the Father and the manner in which human beings come to be related to the Father. For Athanasius, the Father begets his divine Son and so he possesses the Holy Spirit in accord with his divine nature as the Father's Son. The Son, in turn, gives all that he has received to the divine Holy Spirit. This divine interrelationship constitutes the unity of the divine Triad and becomes, within the economy of salvation, the source and goal of the Christian life. Jesus, as the incarnate, Spirit-filled Son, bequeaths to Christians his Holy Spirit, who unites them to him; in being united to Jesus, the Son, they are united to his Father as his adopted, Spirit-filled children. Christians are "made sons through him [the Son] by adoption and grace, as partaking of his Spirit."[8] The divine Triad, then, for Athanasius, is of primary soteriological significance, because the whole point of the Father sending his Son into the world and of the Son pouring out his Holy Spirit upon the world is to ensure that the Father, the Son, and the Holy Spirit, each in their respective manners in accordance with their personal identity, can embrace believers within their very own divine communion of life and love. For Athanasius, this is what it means for human beings to be divinized.

It is important to highlight that, within the above quotation, Athanasius is also arguing that as the Son receives his full divinity from the Father, and so possesses the Holy Spirit by nature, so the Holy Spirit receives his full divinity from the Son and so is divine as the Son himself is divine. The Holy Spirit is fully divine, for he receives from the Son all that the Father has given him, that is, his divinity. While Athanasius is not here advancing Augustine's later understanding that the Holy Spirit proceeds from the Father and the Son (*filioque*)—that is, proceeds as the paternal love of the Father for the Son and as filial love of the Son for the Father—he is giving an active role to the Son in the Father's breathing forth of the Holy Spirit. The Holy Spirit is truly God because he receives from the Son the full divinity that the Father has given to the Son. In this sense, Athanasius does appear to offer a nascent understanding of the *filioque*.[9]

8. Ibid., 3.19. See also Athanasius, *Ad Episcopos Aegypti*, 1.

9. Interestingly, Athanasius's argument is similar to that offered by Augustine and Aquinas, that is, that all that the Spirit possesses from the Father comes through the Son's bestowal. Thus, the Spirit proceeds from the Father and the Son. See Augustine, *De Trinitate*, 15.25–27; and Augustine, *In Evangelium Joannis Tractatus*, 99.8–9. See also, Thomas Aquinas, *Summa Theologiae*, 1.36.2 ad. 1. On this issue of whether or not Athanasius espouses the *filioque*, see Theodore C. Campbell, "The Doc-

The Trinity and the Holy Spirit

Toward the latter part of the Arian controversy, around the year 360, during Athanasius's third exile, a new debate appeared on the horizon. Bishop Serapion of Thmuis, a friend and advocate of Athanasius, wrote to him asking his theological help. A group of Christians, who believed in the full divinity of the Son, denied, nonetheless, that the Holy Spirit was divine. They were known as the *Tropici* because they interpreted the scriptures in a figurative manner. (Later, those who denied the divinity of the Holy Spirit were termed "*Pneumatomachians*"—"Spirit-fighters.") They professed that while the Father and the Son were "alike" in their divinity, the Holy Spirit was "unlike" the Father and the Son and so a creature. The theological grounding for this position was claimed to be Scripture itself, for Scripture never simply calls the Holy Spirit "God." Moreover, a number of scriptures seem to imply that the Spirit was created as one of the angels (see Amos 4:13, 1 Tim 5:21, and Heb 1:14).[10] Furthermore, if the Holy Spirit is divine, it would seem that he would either be another "Son" or, if he proceeded from the Father through the Son, he would be a "grandson." Since both options were untenable, the Holy Spirit must be a creature. Athanasius responded to Serapion by writing four letters wherein he not only refutes the false interpretation of Scripture but, more so, offers a positive scriptural defense and articulation of the Holy Spirit's full divinity.[11]

At the onset of his first letter, Athanasius wants to establish that God is a unified Triad and so develops the argument that we already noted above. As the Arians dishonor the Father by denying the Son, "so also these men [the *Tropici*], in speaking evil of the Holy Spirit, speak evil of the Son."[12] At first glance Athanasius's logic is not so apparent. Only if the divinity of the Holy Spirit is dependent upon the divinity of the Son, as the Son's divinity is dependent upon the divinity of the Father,

trine of the Holy Spirit in the Theology of Athanasius," *Scottish Journal of Theology* 27, no. 4 (1974): 408–40.

10. Athanasius is well aware that the Scripture does not call the Spirit "God" and so never does so himself. Basil the Great will follow this practice as well. The Nicene-Constantinopolitan Creed, while professing the true divinity of the Holy Spirit, will also follow this scriptural tradition and not simply proclaim that the Holy Spirit is "God." It will profess the divinity of the Holy Spirit primarily doxologically: "We believe in the Holy Spirit, the Lord and Giver of life, who proceeds from the Father, who together with the Father and the Son is worshiped and glorified, who spoke through the prophets."
11. For our purposes here, we will focus primarily on Athanasius's first letter to Serapion, for it is the longest and the most scripturally developed and theologically significant.
12. Athanasius, *Ad Serapionem*, 1.1. The translation of Athanasius's *Letters to Serapion* is taken from *The Letters of Saint Athanasius Concerning the Holy Spirit*, trans. C. R. B. Shapland (New York: Philosophical Library, 1951).

is Athanasius's logic sustained. Thus, he argues that "the Spirit of the Son" cannot "be a creature," for as "the Word and the Father" are one, so "the Holy Spirit" shares "the same oneness with the Son as the Son with the Father," and so the Holy Spirit must be divine as the Father and Son are divine. If God is a Triad, then the Father, the Son, and the Holy Spirit must share the same divine nature. To speak correctly of the Word demands that one "think soundly of the Spirit also, who proceeds from the Father, and, belonging to the Word, is from him given to his disciples and all who believe in him."[13] For Athanasius, those who deny the divine status of the Holy Spirit not only deny the divinity of the Son but, ultimately, do not "have the Father," for he would not then be divine either, because he would not be the Father of his only begotten Son.[14] To reject the divinity of the Holy Spirit, according to Athanasius, destroys the ontological interrelationship among the Father, the Son, and the Holy Spirit within the divine Triad.

> For the holy and blessed Triad is indivisible and one in itself. When mention is made of the Father, there is included also his Word, and the Spirit who is in the Son. If the Son is named, the Father is in the Son, and the Spirit is not outside the Word.[15]

Given that the Holy Spirit is truly divine, the unanswered question still remains: why is the Holy Spirit not another Son, or, if the Spirit is from the Son, why is he not then a grandson? Such conclusions can readily be denied as contrary to Scripture and theologically absurd, yet they demand a scriptural and theological explanation. Here, Athanasius lacks a satisfactory answer. To ask such questions is, for Athanasius, to enter into the deep mysteries of God where one is forbidden to travel. Such questions are "impious . . . for it is not fitting to ask such questions about the Godhead. For God is not man, that we should dare to ask human questions about him."[16] The pious response is "to be silent on these matters and disregard these people."[17] For Athanasius, we must content ourselves with the formulas of Scripture and the theological conventions of the tradition, and so acknowledge that the Father, the Son, and the Holy Spirit each possess their own singular identities. Thus, we are assured that within the one divine Triad, "the

13. Ibid., 1.2.
14. Ibid.
15. Ibid., 1.14.
16. Athanasius, *Ad Serapionem*, 1.15.
17. Ibid., 1.16.

Spirit of the Father is called the Spirit of the Son," and in being such, the Spirit is neither the Father nor the Son.[18]

Athanasius, nonetheless, does employ the notion of "image" to help bring light upon this shrouded mystery. "As the Son is in the Spirit, as in his own image, so also the Father is in the Son."[19] As the Son is the "image" of the Father who is manifested in his Son, so the Spirit is the "image" of the Son who is manifested in the Spirit. For Athanasius, the Father, the Son, and the Holy Spirit are mutually co-inhering images; to perceive and know one of them is to perceive and know the others. The notion of a progressive "imaging" does allow Athanasius to maintain the divine triadic unity as well as the distinct identity of the Father, the Son, and the Holy Spirit, for the Son is the begotten image of the Father and the Holy Spirit proceeds as the image of the Son.[20] However, the notion of "image" is significantly flawed on one level. The Son is the image of the Father not only in that he is God as the Father is God but also in that, being the Son, he perfectly reflects the Father. The Son is Son both as to his nature as God and as to his personal identity as Son. The Holy Spirit is the image of the Son only in that he is God as the Son is God, which is Athanasius's main concern. However, the Holy Spirit is not the image of the Son as to his personal identity as the Holy Spirit. The Holy Spirit does not perfectly reflect the Son's sonship as the Son perfectly reflects the Father's fatherhood. While the Son is begotten of the Father, the Spirit is not begotten of the Son. If he were to be begotten of the Son, then he would indeed be a grandson of the Father.[21]

18. Ibid.; see also 1.17, 1.19, and 4.4.
19. Ibid., 1.19.
20. Here again we find Athanasius flirting with the notion of the *filioque*.
21. This issue of what differentiates the Holy Spirit from the Son is really twofold: (1) What is it about the fatherhood of the Father such that he not only begets a Son but also breathes forth a Holy Spirit? (2) What differentiates "the begetting" from "the breathing forth?" The answer to these two questions will determine what differentiates the Son and the Holy Spirit. The Western theological tradition (as found in Augustine and Aquinas) addresses this issue by stating that the Holy Spirit proceeds as the Love of the Father for the Son and as the Love of the Son for the Father, and thus proceeds from the Father and the Son (*filioque*). The Eastern theological tradition has never fully addressed this issue. It does maintain that there is a difference between "the begetting" of the Son and "the proceeding" of the Holy Spirit, but it has never articulated what the difference is. The East traditionally holds that the Spirit proceeds from the Father through the Son. However, it does not formulate how the Spirit's proceeding through the Son affects either the Spirit or the Son. This issue, of course, is one that precipitated the schism between the Eastern and Western churches and one that persists to this day. On this question, see Thomas G. Weinandy, *The Father's Spirit of Sonship: Reconceiving the Trinity* (Edinburgh: T&T Clark: 1995).

Athanasius's Ten Scriptural and Soteriological Proofs for the Spirit's Divinity

In his ongoing contention that the Holy Spirit is indeed truly divine, Athanasius next provides, in his first *Letter to Serapion*, a tenfold series of scriptural arguments. (There is a shorter similar series of these arguments in his third *Letter*.) There are two main thrusts contained in these arguments. First, the Holy Spirit's divinity is grounded in the Spirit's intimate relationship with the Father and Son and so their divine oneness. Second, only if the Holy Spirit is truly divine as the Father and Son are divine can he fulfill, in communion with them, the soteriological tasks scripturally attributed to him.

1. Following upon 1 Corinthians 2:11–12, Athanasius argues:

> For if, as no one knows the things of man save the spirit of man that is in him, so no one knows the things of God save the Spirit of God; would it not be evil speech to call the Spirit who is in God a creature, him who searches even the deep things of God?[22]

Moreover, only if the Spirit is divine can he reveal to believers the salvific truth that is revealed by the Father's Word.

2. Scripture (Ps 104:30, Rom 1:4, 1 Cor 6:11, Titus 3:4–7, and Heb 6:4) professes that the Holy Spirit is the Spirit of holiness and renewal. The Holy Spirit sanctifies and renews creatures, but in order to do so he cannot be a creature himself, but he must possess such holiness as God. As the Son is the creator of all and so is God, so the Holy Spirit who sanctifies also must be God. Likewise, the fruit of the Son's redemption is the work of the divine Holy Spirit, that is, the sanctifying and renewing of all believers and the whole of creation.[23]

3. The Holy Spirit is the "quickening Spirit" (Rom 8:11; John 4:14, 7:39). The Father raises Jesus from the dead through the power of the Holy Spirit, and this same Spirit will raise the mortal bodies of believers back to life. Only if the Spirit shares in the incorruptible divine life of the Father and the Son can he bestow immortality to mortal creatures. "He [the Holy Spirit] that does not partake of life, but who is himself partaken of and quickens the creatures, what kinship can he have with originated beings?"[24]

22. Athanasius, *Ad Serapionem*, 1.22.
23. Ibid., 1.23.
24. Ibid.

4. The Holy Spirit is also "called unction and seal" (Isa 61:1, Gal 4:29, 2 Cor 2:15, Eph 1:13, and 2 Pet 1:4). Because it is the Word who anoints and seals through the Holy Spirit, the seal of the Holy Spirit comprises "the form of Christ who seals," and because of this, believers "share in the same divine nature," for they partake "of the Word in the Spirit."[25] We see again that, for Athanasius, Christians are divinized precisely because, through the indwelling of the divine Spirit, they are in communion with the divine Word.

5. Athanasius immediately emphasizes this same point from another perspective. Christians are temples of the Holy Spirit and so "become partakers of God." The seal of the Holy Spirit belongs "to the nature of the Son who, through the Spirit who is in him, joins us to the Father." Thus, the Spirit cannot be a creature but is of "the nature of God" for "the Father, through the Word, in the Holy Spirit, creates and renews all things."[26]

6. Significantly, Athanasius argues for the divinity of the Holy Spirit by accentuating that the Son and the Spirit act in communion with one another. Together, they collaborate in bringing about the salvation of Christians. To intensify this divine unity of the Son and Holy Spirit working in tandem with one another, Athanasius speaks again of the Holy Spirit being "the image of the Son." "For as the image is, so also must be that who is its image."[27] This image, however, resides solely in the Holy Spirit being truly divine as the Son is divine and not insofar as the Holy Spirit reflects the Son's sonship. "If the Son, because he is of the Father, is proper to his essence, it must be that the Spirit, who is said to be from God, is in essence proper to the Son."[28] Moreover, because the Spirit shares in the same divine nature as the Son, "the Holy Spirit is called the Spirit of Sonship." Therefore, "as the Son is wisdom and truth, this Spirit is described as Spirit of wisdom and truth. Again, the Son is the power of God and the Lord of Glory, and the Spirit is called Spirit of power and glory."[29] For Athanasius, while the Word, as the Father's Son, *is* wisdom, truth, power, and glory, the Spirit, being the Spirit of sonship is the Spirit *of* wisdom, truth, power, and glory, for the Son has conferred upon the Spirit all that he has received from the Father. Once more, we see that, for Athanasius, the Son is instrumental

25. Ibid.
26. Ibid., 1.24.
27. Ibid.
28. Ibid., 1.25.
29. Ibid.

in constituting the Spirit's divinity by sharing with the Spirit all of the Father's divine attributes.

7. Similarly, as the Son shares in the Father's unchangeable divine nature so "the Holy Spirit, being in God, must be incapable of change, variation, and corruption."[30]

8. Likewise, as God is everywhere, so "the Spirit of the Lord fills the universe." Creatures, even angels, are "circumscribed," but the Spirit, as is the Word, is present with and "fills all things."[31]

9. Athanasius highlights once again that "the Holy Spirit is partaken of and does not partake." The Holy Spirit is "always the same," and he, being proper to the Word, empowers believers to partake of what is of God and so not a creature who partakes of God.[32]

10. Athanasius concludes by noting that "the Holy Spirit is one, but the creatures are many." "Because the Spirit is one, and, still more, because he is proper to the Word who is one, he is proper to God who is one, and one in essence (*homoousion*) with him."[33] Here, Athanasius is unafraid to call upon Nicaea's strategic, and controversial, term.[34] He does so to enhance and ensure the Spirit's oneness with the Father and the Son. He is able to do so because he grasps that as the Son is proper to the Father's essence and so *homoousion* with the Father, so the Spirit is proper to the Word/Son's essence and so also *homoousion* with the Father. For Athanasius, the Father, the Son, and the Holy Spirit are all one and the same God, "the Holy Triad."[35]

Tradition and the Spirit's Divinity

Having finished his soteriological scriptural arguments for the Spirit's full divinity, Athanasius proceeds to invoke the constant tradition of the faith within the Catholic Church, the faith that was given to the apostles and professed by all of the fathers.[36] Athanasius summarizes

30. Ibid., 1.26. Athanasius refers to Wis 1:5, 12:1; 1 Cor 2:11; 1 Pet 3:4; and Jas 1:17.
31. Athanasius, *Ad Serapionem*, 1.26. Athanasius references Ps 139:7 and Wis 12:1.
32. Athanasius, *Ad Serapionem*, 1.27.
33. Ibid.
34. The only other occasion where Athanasius states that the Holy Spirit is *homoousion* with the Father and the Son is in *Ad Serapionem*, 3.1. In keeping with Scripture, both Athanasius and Basil the Great never refer to the Holy Spirit as God. However, unlike Athanasius, Basil the Great, in his *On the Holy Spirit*, also never states that the Holy Spirit is *homoousion* with the Father and the Son. Conversely, Gregory of Nazianzus, impatient with Basil's reluctance, adamantly affirms both that the Spirit is God and that he is *homoousion* with the Father and the Son. See Gregory of Nazianzus, *Oratio*, 31.10.
35. Athanasius, *Ad Serapionem*, 1.27.
36. See ibid., 1.28–30.

that faith by providing his most comprehensive testament to the Holy Triad.

> There is, then, a Triad, holy and complete, confessed to be in Father, Son and Holy Spirit, having nothing foreign or external mixed with it, not composed of one that creates and one that is originated, but all creative and constructive; and it is consistent in itself and indivisible in nature, and its activity is one. For the Father does all things through the Word and the Holy Spirit; thus the unity of the holy Triad is preserved.[37]

Athanasius distinguishes the singular identities of the Father, the Son, and the Holy Spirit as well as simultaneously acknowledging their unity of nature. While they act as the one God, the Father acts through the distinct actions of the Son and the Holy Spirit.

Athanasius then returns to the sacrament of baptism. No one can be baptized in the Father alone, or the Son alone, or the Father and the Son, for without the Holy Spirit one is not taken up into the very life of God as God truly is, and so would not be truly divinized. "For as baptism, which is given in the Father, Son and Holy Spirit, is one; and as there is one faith in the Triad; so also the Holy Triad." Thus, Athanasius confirms that without the Holy Spirit, Christians possess no union with the Father and the Son. "For it is when we partake of him [the Holy Spirit] that we have the love of the Father, the grace of the Son, and the communion of the Spirit himself."[38] So Athanasius concludes his first *Letter*: "True worshipers, therefore, worship the Father, but in Spirit and Truth, confessing the Son and in him the Spirit. For the Spirit is inseparable from the Son, as the Son is inseparable from the Father."[39] For Athanasius, to deny the divinity of the Holy Spirit is to blaspheme him and so commit, as Jesus warned, the unforgivable sin.

Conclusion

The source of Athanasius's defense and articulation of the Trinity and, specifically, that of the divinity of the Holy Spirit is Scripture itself, for it proclaims that the one God is the Father, the Son, and the Holy Spirit. This is what the church has always professed and proclaimed. For Athanasius, as the Father is eternally the Father of the Son, so the Holy Spirit must be the eternal Spirit of the Father and the Son. As

37. Ibid., 1.28.
38. Ibid., 1.30.
39. Ibid., 1.33.

the Father and Son mutually co-inhere in one another, so the Son and Holy Spirit must mutually co-inhere in one another, and so, in turn, the Holy Spirit must mutually co-inhere in the Father. This ontological communion of being and action between the Father, the Son, and the Holy Spirit is the defining characteristic of Athanasius's theology of the Holy Spirit and, ultimately, of the Trinity itself. In this mutual ontological interrelationship among the Father, the Son, and the Holy Spirit, Athanasius offered the theological foundation for the future notion of their *perichoresis*, that is, their mutual intercommunion and co-inherence. Thus, Athanasius advanced the church's understanding of the Trinity, both in the East and the West, in a significant manner that continues to today.

3

Athanasius's Incarnational Soteriology

We have seen in the previous two chapters that Athanasius championed the full divinity of the Son and the Holy Spirit and, in so doing, confirmed that the one God is the Father, the Son, and the Holy Spirit. Athanasius did so believing that such was the authentic faith of the church founded upon the apostles, professed in the Scriptures, and confirmed within the subsequent theological tradition. In the midst of all this, soteriology was not far from Athanasius's mind. Only if the Son was truly God did God truly become a human being and, in so doing, secure our salvation through his human life, death, and resurrection. Moreover, only if the fruit of the Son's redemption was the truly divine Holy Spirit could human beings actually be taken into the very life and love of the Father and the Son and so be genuinely divinized. In this chapter, we will examine Athanasius's soteriological Christology. Within the incarnation, Athanasius perceives the full significance of the divinity of the Father, the Son, and the Holy Spirit, for in the Son becoming a human being and obtaining humankind's salvation, we see the saving love of God the Father, the salvific work of his Son, and the abundant outpouring of the Holy Spirit.

Athanasius and the Three Incarnational Truths

By way of introducing Athanasius's soteriological Christology, we need to understand clearly the inherent incarnational issues at hand so as to grasp the importance of his response to them. Athanasius instinctively knew through faith that to conceive and articulate the incarnation properly, one needed to uphold three truths simultaneously. While he would not have stated them in this manner, the following are these three incarnational truths. First, it must *truly be God* who came to exist in the flesh. We already observed this in Athanasius's defense of the Nicene doctrine that the Son is God as the Father is God. Second, the divine Son must be *fully human*. Here, the emphasis is on the full and authentic humanity of Jesus. As we will see, some scholars believe that Athanasius failed to uphold this incarnational truth. However, we will find that this interpretation is not in keeping with Athanasius's actual thought. Third, the divine Son of God must *truly be* a genuine human being. This truth highlights that the union between the Son's divinity and his true humanity must be such that the Son actually *exists* as one of us. The union cannot be a moral union such as is found in the proposal that the Son only adopted the man Jesus through the Holy Spirit. Jesus would then be similar to other holy people and prophets, even if he is the paramount holy person and the supreme prophet. Athanasius recognizes that Jesus is the Son of God existing in a human manner, and, as we will see, he does so in a very significant manner—his use of what is termed "the communication of idioms."

By way of commencing his soteriological Christology, the following quotation exemplifies Athanasius articulating these three incarnational truths:

> For man, if joined to a creature, was not deified, unless the Son were truly God; nor was man brought into the Father's presence unless he had been his natural and true Word who had put on the body. And as we would not have been delivered from sin and the curse, unless it had been human flesh by nature that the Word put on (for there should be nothing common to us with what is foreign), so also the man would not have been deified unless the Word who became flesh had been by nature from the Father and true and proper to him. Therefore the union was of this kind, that he might unite what is man by nature to him who is of the nature of the Godhead, and his salvation and deification might be sure. Therefore let those who deny that the Son is from the Father by nature and proper to his *ousia*, deny also that he took true human flesh from the ever-virgin

> Mary; for in neither case would it have been of profit to us men, whether the Word were not true and naturally Son of God, or the flesh not true which he assumed.[1]

Athanasius ardently wishes to ensure that human beings are truly divinized. To ensure this, he emphasizes that the Son must be truly God, for only if such is the case can genuine divinization take place. Moreover, the Son must assume an authentic humanity, for only in such an assumption is the assumed full humanity divinized. Likewise, the union between the Son's divinity and his humanity must be such that they are one, for only if the Son *exists* humanly can his humanity, and thus all human beings, be actually taken up into the divine life of his Father. With the above in mind, we can now proceed to examine more closely Athanasius's soteriological Christology.

What Does It Mean for the Word to "Become" Flesh?

To possess a proper understanding of the incarnation, it is essential, for Athanasius, to grasp the proper meaning of John 1:14: "The Word became flesh." The crucial task here is to define the word *become*. Athanasius is very clear on what *become* does not mean.

> He became man, and did not come into man; for this is necessary to know, lest these irreligious men fall into this notion also, and beguile any into thinking that, as in former times the Word was used to come into each of the saints, so now he sojourned in a man, hallowing him also, and manifesting himself as he had in others. . . . Of old he came to the saints individually, and hallowed those who rightly received him; but neither was it said that when they were begotten that he had become man, nor, when they suffered that he himself suffered.[2]

Athanasius insists that the Word of God actually came to exist in a human manner and did not simply come to dwell in a human being as the Word of God came upon and dwelt in previous holy people. In these former manifestations of the Word, the Word merely inspired people who lived holy lives and spoke his word. For Athanasius, the terminus of the incarnational "becoming" was his actual existence in the flesh, and it is precisely because he existed humanly that all that pertained to his humanity can be attributed to him, such as human suffering.

1. Athanasius, *Contra Arianos*, 2.70; see also 2.69.
2. Athanasius, *Contra Arianos*, 3.30–31. See also Athanasius, *Tomus ad Antiochenos*, 7; and Athanasius, *Ad Adelphium*, 11.

Thus, the incarnational "becoming" expresses an ontological "becoming," that is, that the Word, in "becoming" flesh, "comes to exist" as a human being.

If the Son of God did not simply "come into a man" but actually "became man," does that not mean that the Word of God changed in so becoming human as the Arians supposed, confirming that the Word/Son is not truly divine, for God cannot change? Does not the concept of *becoming* by its very nature demand change? Athanasius insists that the Son of God, being God, did not change in becoming flesh, nor, in becoming flesh, did he change into flesh. In order to avoid *becoming* meaning some form of change, Athanasius consistently adds such phrases as "taking on flesh," "putting on flesh," and "entering into flesh."[3] The incarnational *becoming* is not the Word changing in some manner, much less changing into something that he previously was not. Rather, in becoming human, the Son positively takes on a new manner of existence; that is, while remaining God, he now comes to exist as a human being by ontologically "taking on" or "putting on" human flesh. In his letter to Epictetus, bishop of Corinth, Athanasius maintains that "he [the Son] has become flesh not by being changed into flesh, but because he assumed living flesh on our behalf, and has become man."[4]

There are two theological, interrelated reasons for why the incarnational notion of *become* does not mean "change into." First, Athanasius realizes that to attribute change to God would mean that he could either become better or worse through the changes he undergoes, such as changes that occur within human beings. But God, by definition, is perfect in every way and so he cannot change for the better, nor could he, being perfectly good and loving, change for the worse. Therefore, the Son of God cannot change if he is to be perfectly God as the Father is God. Second, Athanasius recognizes that the Son of God must remain perfectly who he is as the all-good and loving God in becoming a human being for the sake of the incarnation. If the Son of God changed in becoming a human being, then it would no longer be the perfect Son of God who now existed as one of us, but a lesser form of himself. Moreover, if the Son of God actually did change into flesh, then it would no longer be the Son of God who is flesh but simply a human being who once was the Son of God. For Athanasius, the incarnational *becoming* is not like the caterpillar changing into a butterfly, whereby the caterpillar ceases to be and the butterfly comes to be.[5]

3. See Athanasius, *Contra Arianos*, 2.8, 47; 3.29, 31–32, 34; and Athanasius, *Ad Adelphium*, 7.
4. Athanasius, *Ad Epictetum*, 8. See also ibid., 2.

The Communications of Idioms

Arius and his followers assembled a battery of scriptural passages that appear to confirm that the Son/Word was a creature. Proverbs 8:22 is the most legendary: "The Lord created me at the beginning of his work, the first of his acts of long ago."[6] But there are many others they appealed to in order to make their point, for example: "the firstborn within a large family" (Rom 8:29); "the first born of all creation" (Col 1:15); "the Father is greater than I" (John 14:28). They also marshalled all of the passages that ascribed ignorance, weakness, suffering, and growth to Jesus, the Son of God. While Athanasius, in various ways, addressed all of these passages in his anti-Arian writings, his predominant method in refuting them, especially those that attributed various forms of weakness and growth to Jesus, was to make a critical distinction. Following the already existing tradition, Athanasius insisted that such characteristics as suffering, ignorance, and growth were predicated of the Son not insofar as he is God but insofar as he is human. What the Arians failed to grasp was the truth of the incarnation, and so, in Athanasius's view, they were similar to the Jews. "For the Jews said; 'How, being man, can he be God?' And the Arians, 'If he were very God from God, how could he become man?'. . . Thus both parties deny the eternity and Godhead of the Word in consequence of those human attributes which the Savior took to him by reason of the flesh which he bore."[7] For Athanasius, "all these texts have the same force and meaning, a religious one, demonstrative of the divinity of the Word, even those of them which speak humanly concerning him, as having become the Son of man."[8] The Arians were "ignorant" of the "scope of faith which Christians hold, and using it as a rule, apply themselves . . . to reading the inspired Word."[9]

> Now the scope and character of Scripture, as we have often said, is this: it contains a double account of the Savior, that he is ever God and is Son,

5. What Athanasius is grappling with is the singular manner in which the Gospel of John employs the word *become*. *Become* normally, by definition, denotes some form of change. However, within the incarnation it is employed in a new one-off manner, in a manner that was never used before and never will be used again, the reason being that never before did one being, God, become another being, a human being, without ceasing to be who he always was, God. The incarnational *become* does not imply a change in the Word's existence as God but denotes his assuming a human manner of existence so as to actually exist as a human being.
6. Scripture quotations are taken from the New Revised Standard Version.
7. Athanasius, *Contra Arianos*, 3.27.
8. Ibid., 2.1.
9. Ibid., 3.28; see also 1.59; 2.12, 75.

> the Father's Word and Radiance and Wisdom; and that afterwards he took flesh for us of the Virgin, Mary the Bearer of God (*Theotokos*), and was made man. This scope is to be found throughout the God-inspired Scripture.[10]

For Athanasius, it is one and the same divine Son who exists eternally as God and who came to exist in time as a human being, and, therefore, both divine and human predicates can properly be attributed to him. This is the rule of what has come to be called the communication of idioms.

> Indeed, one [being] is signified from both, for "the Word was made flesh." But the expressions employed regarding his Godhead, and those regarding his becoming man, are to be interpreted with discrimination and suitably to the particular context. He that writes of the human attributes of the Word knows also what concerns his Godhead, and he who exegetes concerning his Godhead is not ignorant of what belongs to his coming in the flesh.[11]

Because the incarnational *become* means neither the Son's dwelling in a human person nor his changing into human flesh but his coming to exist in a truly human manner, all that is truly proper to being a human being can rightly be predicated of him. For Athanasius, the Son is ontologically united to his humanity and, therefore, lived an authentic human life.

> And as we said that he [the Son/Word] suffered in the flesh, hungered in the flesh, and was fatigued in the flesh, so may he also reasonably be said to have advanced in the flesh; for neither did the advance, such as we have described it, take place with the Word external to the flesh, for in him was the flesh which advanced.[12]

Significantly, for Athanasius, the above understanding is critical for our salvation. Because the Word assumed corruptible flesh from Mary, it is necessary that

> suffering and weeping and toiling, these things which are proper to the flesh, are ascribed to him together with the body. If then he wept and was troubled, it was not the Word, as being the Word who wept and was troubled, but it was proper to the flesh. If he also pleaded that "the cup might

10. Ibid., 3.29.
11. Athanasius, *De Sententia Dionysii*, 9.
12. Athanasius, *Contra Arianos*, 3.53; see also 2.11–13, 3.54–55.

> pass away," it was not the Godhead that was in terror, but this passion too was proper to the manhood. And the words "Why hast thou forsaken me?" are his, according to the explanation offered above, though he suffered nothing, for the Word was impassible. This is nonetheless declared by the evangelists, since the Lord became man and these things are done and said as from a man, that he might himself lighten these sufferings of the flesh, and free it from them.[13]

While the Son of God was impassible as God, and so could not suffer and die, for our sake and for our salvation the Son became a human being, taking upon himself humankind's suffering and death so that he might free humankind from the suffering of sin and death. For Athanasius, to deny that the divine Son of God truly suffered and died as one of us, as an authentic human being, is to deprive us of salvation.

Athanasius's ardent defense and his clear exposition of the legitimacy of communications of idioms demonstrate that he fully grasped the three theological truths necessary for a proper understanding of the incarnation, for the communication of idioms entails these very truths. First, to predicate weakness, ignorance, suffering, and death to the Son of God demands that it actually be the divine Son of God who became human, for if it was not actually the Father's only-begotten Son who became flesh, such truths could not be predicated of him. Second, to predicate undisputable human attributes to the Son demands that the Son existed in a fully, genuinely human manner, for if he was not truly human, he could not be born of Mary, suffer, and die. Third, only if the Son of God actually ontologically existed as a human being, and did not merely dwell in a human being, could the Son actually experience all that was indisputably human and act in an authentic human manner. For Athanasius, only in upholding these three incarnational truths is one able to sustain the salvation that the incarnation achieved.

However, at this point, one of the most controverted contemporary issues surrounding Athanasius's understanding of the incarnation arises. Did Athanasius believe that Jesus possessed a human soul, and so did he really sustain the full humanity of the Son of God?

13. Ibid., 3.56; see also 2.16 and 3.26.

The Human Soul of Christ

Many contemporary theologians argue that Athanasius did not posit a human soul in Jesus. While a few have defended Athanasius, the consensus has been that his Christology does not make any provision for a soul, and if he later does admit a soul after the Synod of Alexandria in 362, he gives it no soteriological significance. Such a criticism is unwarranted and misses one of the fundamental points of Athanasius's Christology.[14]

While he often uses the term *flesh*, following the prologue of John's Gospel, Athanasius specifies that it is "the custom of Scripture to call man by the name 'flesh,'" citing Joel 2:28 and Daniel 14:5.[15] He also acknowledges that "to say 'the Word became flesh' is equivalent to saying 'the Word became man.'"[16] Moreover, in accordance with the Greek understanding of *sarx* (flesh), Athanasius perceives all of the weaknesses and frailties that pertain to human beings. He does so precisely to accentuate the frail and weak humanity of the divine Son, and so his likeness to all other human beings. Soteriologically this is essential, for only if the Son lives an authentic human life, even unto suffering and death, is humankind saved.

Critics admit that Athanasius never denies that Christ had a soul, but they note that in arguing against the Arians, who deny the Son's divinity precisely because of these human weaknesses, Athanasius never argues that such frailties reside in his soul and not within his impassible divinity. Such an argument, the critics claim, would have helped Athanasius's cause. This may be true, but what the critics miss is Athanasius's deeper christological and soteriological concerns. For Athanasius, while the Son of God did not suffer defects, such as ignorance and fear, within his divinity, a true understanding of the incarnation did demand, for soteriological reasons, that it was truly the Son

14. A full bibliography of the controversy cannot be given here; for a full bibliography, see Weinandy, *Athanasius*, 91. It should be noted, nonetheless, that this criticism of Athanasius was popularized by Aloys Grillmeier. He divided the early fathers by whether or not they ascribed a human soul to Christ. Those who did he classified as presenting a *Logos-Anthropos* (Word-Man) Christology, and those who did not he classified as offering a *Logos-Sarx* (Word-Flesh) Christology. He wrongly lumped Athanasius into the last category, along with Apollinarius and Cyril of Alexandria. While Apollinarius did deny that Jesus had a human soul, the real problem is Grillmeier's specious hermeneutical template. It is erroneous to attempt to classify all of the fathers by their stance over the issue of Christ's "soul." Rather, the fathers must be judged over whether or not they uphold the three incarnational truths that were discussed above. See Aloys Grillmeier, *Christ in Christian Tradition*, vol. 1, *From the Apostolic Age to Chalcedon (451)*, trans. J. S. Bowden (London: Mowbray, 1975), 308–28.
15. Athanasius, *Contra Arianos*, 3.30.
16. Athanasius, *Ad Epictetum*, 8.

of God who suffered the weaknesses of his humanity. Athanasius held that the incarnation demanded that the Son "in putting on human flesh . . . put it on whole with the passions proper to it."[17] In putting on the whole flesh, the Son assumed all that was proper to the whole of his humanity, not simply the passions that pertained to the body but those that pertained to the body and soul, the complete nature—"hunger," "fatigue," "terror," and "abandonment." Such passions are not merely physical but also contain the emotions of the intellect and will. This is why Athanasius laid such great stress on the communication of idioms. "When the flesh suffered the Word was not external to it . . . and when he did his Father's works divinely, the flesh was not external to him, but in the body itself did the Lord do them."[18] Athanasius was not fearful, then, of attributing ignorance to Jesus—clearly a defect of the intellectual soul.

> The Word as man was ignorant of [the last day], for ignorance is proper to man, and especially ignorance of these things. Moreover, this is proper to the Saviour's love of man, for since he was made man he was not ashamed, on account of the flesh which is ignorant, to say "I know not," so that he may show that while knowing as God, he is ignorant according to the flesh.[19]

What needs to be noticed in this selection is that Athanasius not only affirms that the Son suffers humanly but that when he performs his divine deeds, his miracles, the Son performs them humanly as well. As the incarnate Son, Jesus did not do divine deeds *in* a human being, as if some actions were merely human and some actions, the important ones, were done divinely apart from his humanity. When Jesus healed Peter's mother-in-law, "he stretched forth his hand humanly, but he stopped the illness divinely."[20] What Athanasius is accentuating is what later would be called Jesus's *theandric* acts, that is, divine deeds done humanly. This is soteriologically significant. For Athanasius, Jesus achieved our salvation precisely as the Son of God, but he performed his saving acts in a human manner, humanly offering his human life on the cross for our salvation.

17. Athanasius, *Ad Epictetum*, 3.32.
18. Ibid.
19. Ibid., 3.43.
20. Ibid., 3.32. The same is true of Jesus healing the blind man by placing his spittle on the man's eyes and Jesus using his human voice in calling Lazarus forth from the tomb. See ibid.; Athanasius, *De Sententia Dionysii*, 9; Athanasius, *Tomus ad Antiochus*, 7; and Athanasius, *Ad Adelphium*, 3.

> When we see him doing or saying anything divinely, through the instrument of his own body, we may know that being God he [Jesus] so works, and also, if we see him speaking and suffering humanly, we may not be ignorant that bearing flesh he became man, and hence so acts and speaks. For if we recognize what is proper to each, we see and understand that both these things are done by one.[21]

For Athanasius, Jesus is the "one" incarnate divine Son who is the sole actor within all of the human salvific deeds he performs, whether he is preaching to the crowds or multiplying the loaves.

In the light of all of the above, it is not surprising that Athanasius endorses, contrary to his critics, the Council of Alexandria in 362, which condemned the notion that Jesus did not have a soul and affirmed that he was fully human as we are human, constituted as a human being with both a body and a soul.

> For they [the fathers of the council] confessed also that the Saviour had not only a body without a soul, nor without sense or intelligence; for it was impossible, when the Lord had become man for us, that his body should be without intelligence; nor was salvation effected in the Word himself a salvation of body only, but of soul as well.[22]

In a similar manner, Athanasius writes to Epictetus, saying that the Son assumed a whole humanity, for "the salvation of the whole man was brought about. . . . [And salvation does not] extend to the body only, but the whole man, body and soul."[23] In both passages, Athanasius is significantly anticipating the maxim of Gregory of Nazianzus that "what is not assumed is not healed," and, therefore, the Son of God had to assume the whole of human nature, body and soul, if he was to save the whole of our humanity.[24]

Athanasius's Christology, founded upon the teaching of Scripture and the tradition of the church, was immensely influential. Cyril of Alexandria would appropriate and develop all of Athanasius's principal incarnational tenets. When confronted with Nestorius's denial that Mary should be called the Mother of God, *Theotokos*, with the implication that the Son of God was not truly born of her, Cyril championed the validity of the communication of idioms. If the Son of God was truly conceived within Mary's womb as a human being through the power

21. Athanasius, *Contra Arianos*, 3.35; see also 3.31.
22. Athanasius, *Tomus ad Antiochenos*, 7.
23. Athanasius, *Ad Epictetum*, 7.
24. Gregory of Nazianzus, *Epistula*, 101.7.

of the Holy Spirit, and thus truly born of her, then she can rightly and truly be called the Mother of God. To deny that Mary is the Mother of God is tantamount, for Cyril, to denying the incarnation. Cyril realized, as did his mentor Athanasius, that the communication of idioms embodied all three incarnational truths—that it was *truly the divine Son* who *truly existed* as an *authentic human being*, and thus that divine and human attributes are rightly predicated of him who is the Son of God. Cyril's Christology, in turn, resides at the heart of the Council of Chalcedon (451). Within the creed of the council, then, one can distinctly perceive the evident echo of Athanasius. The council, in upholding the full divinity and humanity of Jesus as the Son of God incarnate, professed in its first paragraph:

> Following therefore the holy Fathers [of the Council of Nicaea], we unanimously teach to confess one and the same Son, our Lord Jesus Christ, the same perfect in divinity and perfect in humanity, the same truly God and truly man composed of rational soul and body, the same one in being [*homoousion*] with the Father as to his divinity and one in being [*homoousion*] with us as to the humanity, like unto us in all things but sin. The same begotten from the Father before the ages as to the divinity and in the latter days for us and our salvation was born as to his humanity from Mary the Virgin Mother of God [*Theotokos*].[25]

For Chalcedon, as it was for Athanasius, it is "one and the same" Son who exists perfectly as God as the Father is God and exists perfectly as a human being as we do, and therefore, that "same" divine Son was truly born of Mary for our salvation. This profession of faith continues to be proclaimed to this day, and in consequence, Athanasius's soteriological Christology still resounds.

Salvation—Being Deified in Christ

We have seen throughout our examination of Athanasius's Christology that soteriology resides at its heart. Only if Jesus is truly the Son of God who truly exists as an authentic human being is salvation assured. This is witnessed to profoundly in the following passage:

> For he [the Son] suffered to prepare freedom from suffering for those who suffer in him. He descended that he might raise up, he went down to corruption, that corruption might put on immortality, he became weak for

25. Translation taken from Denzinger, *Compendium of Creeds*, no. 301; see also no. 302.

> us, that we might rise with power, he descended to death, that he might bestow on us immortality, and gave life to the dead. Finally, he became man, that we who die as men might live again, and that death should no more reign over us.[26]

For Athanasius, the Father foresaw this work of salvation though his Son from before the foundation of the world, and so his Son's incarnation was eternally predestined. The Father not only created humankind through his Word but also "prior to us is the repair of our salvation founded in Christ, that in him we might be new-created."[27] Moreover, in becoming incarnate, Jesus himself must first progress in perfection and so be deified so that, by our being united to him, we might be deified in him. Jesus's "manhood advanced in wisdom, transcending by degrees human nature, being deified and becoming and appearing to all as the organ of wisdom for the operation and the shining forth of the Godhead."[28] For Athanasius, Jesus's baptism was an event whereby Jesus was further sanctified, and in being so, he was able to make us holy. "When he is baptised, we it is who are baptised . . . for he sanctifies himself that we might be sanctified in him."[29] This process of deification finds its culmination in Jesus's death and resurrection, for in these saving acts Jesus conquers all that is not of God, as well as sin and death, and assumes the fullness of the divine life of the Holy Spirit. The Son came to dwell in Adam's sinful flesh so that "sin might be perfectly expelled from the flesh."[30] "Therefore, the perfect Word of God puts around himself an imperfect body, and is said to be 'created for the works'; that paying the debt in our stead, he might in himself perfect what was wanting in man."[31] Jesus becomes, in his resurrection, the "firstborn" of many brothers and sisters, for he is the first to reap the fruit of his own redemption and, in so doing, is able to share this fruit with those who abide in him.

> His flesh was saved and liberated before all others, as being the Word's body; henceforth we, becoming incorporated with it, are saved after that pattern. . . . He was the first to rise, as man, raising his body for our sakes. Henceforth, since he is risen, we, too, from him and through him rise in due course from the dead.[32]

26. Athanasius, *Festal Letter*, 10.8.
27. Athanasius, *Contra Arianos*, 3.77. Athanasius is commenting on Eph 1:3–5. See also Athanasius, *Contra Arianos*, 3.67.
28. Athanasius, *Contra Arianos*, 3.53.
29. Ibid., 1.48.
30. Ibid., 2.56; see also 1.43, 1.59–60.
31. Ibid., 2.66.

In Christ, humankind is restored not only to the dignity it possessed at the dawn of creation but now, through Christ, "with yet greater grace," for it will now reign with him forever in the heavens.[33] As Jesus became incorruptible at his resurrection, so "it is clear that the resurrection of all of us will take place; and since his body remained without corruption, there can be no doubt regarding our incorruption."[34] The risen Jesus accomplishes this incorruptible deification through the Holy Spirit for he became Lord "in order to hallow all by the Spirit."[35] In Christ through his Spirit human beings become "sons and gods," for they "were adopted and deified through the Word."[36] To be deified is then to be taken into, and so to share in, the very interrelational life of the Trinity.

> For since the Word is in the Father, and the Spirit is given from the Word, he wills that we should receive the Spirit, that when we receive it, thus having the Spirit of the Word which is in the Father, we too may be found, on account of the Spirit, to become one with the Word, and through him in the Father.[37]

For Athanasius, this is the whole purpose of the incarnation. The Son of God ultimately became "man that he might deify us in himself . . . and [so make us] 'partakers of the divine nature,' as Peter wrote."[38] Early in his theological career, Athanasius already summarized the whole of his soteriological Christology. "He [the Son] was made man that we might be made God; and he manifested himself by a body that we might receive the idea of the unseen Father; and he endured the insolence of men that we might inherit immortality."[39]

Antony—the Perfect Image of Christ

In closing our study of Athanasius's soteriological Christology, we should briefly consider his *Life of Antony*, because in Athanasius's view Antony was the epitome of what it means to live a deified life in Christ. In abandoning his life in the world and hiding himself in the desert, Antony gradually assumed the image of Christ. He did this through

32. Ibid., 2.61; see also 2.64.
33. Ibid., 2.67.
34. Athanasius, *Festal Letter*, 11.14. See also, Athanasius, *Contra Arianos*, 3.58.
35. Athanasius, *Contra Arianos*, 2.14; see also 2.18.
36. Ibid., 1.39; see also 1.38, 43; 3.19.
37. Ibid., 3.25; see also 3.24; Athanasius, *De Decretis*, 14.
38. Athanasius, *Ad Adelphium*, 4.
39. Athanasius, *De Incarnatione*, 54.3. See also Athanasius, *Contra Arianos*, 2.10.

constant prayer, turning away from sin, acquiring the holy life of virtue through fasting and discipline, and, above all, through growing in love for his neighbor and for the Lord Jesus himself. In the midst of his Spirit-filled striving, the devil was ever close at hand, tempting Antony with the allurements of the world and the flesh. "But the enemy saw his own weakness in the face of Anthony's resolve. . . . Working with Anthony was the Lord, who bore flesh for us, and gave to the body victory over the devil, so that each of those who truly struggle can say, it *is not I, but the grace of God which is in me.*"[40]

When people later came to Antony, they found a man who had been recreated in Christ, the new Adam, for he truly knew and loved God and his neighbor. He lived a truly rational life, having been renewed in the Spirit, with all of his emotional and intellectual desires attuned to truth and love.

> The state of his was one of purity, for it was not constrained by grief, nor relaxed by pleasure, nor affected by either laughter or dejection. Moreover, when he saw the crowd, he was not annoyed any more than he was elated at being embraced by so many people. He maintained utter equilibrium, like one guided by reason and steadfast in that which accords with nature. Through him the Lord healed many of those present who suffered from bodily ailments; others purged of demons, and to Anthony he gave the grace of speech. Thus he consoled many who mourned, and others hostile to each other he reconciled in friendship, urging everyone to prefer nothing in the world above the love of Christ.[41]

For Athanasius, Antony had become truly deified in Christ and thus lived in full communion with the Father through the Holy Spirit. In so doing, he lived in love with all of his brothers and sisters in Christ.

40. Athanasius, *Vita Antonii*, 30.
41. Ibid., 14.

PART II

The Contested Legacy of Athanasius

Introduction

> Athanasius of Alexandria has divided modern opinion just as surely as he divided those of his contemporaries.[1]
>
> —David Gwynn

From the start, conflict and contention have encompassed the figure of Athanasius. The epithet commonly employed in praise of Athanasius, *contra mundum* (against the world), aptly reflects the struggle that has beset him from his day until ours. Upon his elevation as Alexandria's archbishop in 328 CE he became embroiled in disputes on several fronts. He was driven from his see five times, spending upward of seventeen years in exile. Throughout the forty-six years of his episcopal ministry, whether through personal contact or the written word, Athanasius combined a fierce defense of his conduct with a sharp refutation of those he termed "Arians," all the while explicating the Trinitarian-incarnational account of the Christian faith that he championed. As the time of his death drew near (in 373), resident in his own city of Alexandria, he found relative peace, having been reconciled with many of his former opponents and able to see the impending triumph of the Nicene faith on the horizon.

A microcosm of the contested legacy of Athanasius appears in early

1. David M. Gwynn, *Athanasius of Alexandria: Bishop, Theologian, Ascetic, Father* (Oxford: Oxford University Press, 2012), 195.

fifth-century church histories. The dominant interpretation, wholly favorable to Athanasius, appears in Socrates, Sozomen, and Theodoret.[2] These church historians, writing between 439 and 450, recount the history of Athanasius's struggles in great detail and judge him entirely innocent of all charges against him. In the words of Theodoret, Athanasius was "the champion of the truth." "Athanasius very rapidly acquired legendary status as the one who defended Nicene orthodoxy pretty well single-handed through the years of Arian ascendency."[3] The minority view, highly critical of Athanasius's conduct and teaching, is espoused by Philostorgius (d. ca. 439), a strong supporter of the teaching of Aetius and Eunomius.[4] These divergent readings of Athanasius's teaching and character will be replicated and further developed in the modern period. Notwithstanding this early contention over Athanasius's legacy, the Eastern and Western Christian traditions have received Athanasius enthusiastically as the champion of Christian orthodoxy and the supreme exemplar—the icon—of the struggle for the faith against all odds. Any account of Athanasius's reception must take into account this iconic—and sometimes hotly contested—role he played in a hugely pivotal era for the church.

The task of tracing the reception of Athanasius faces two notable challenges with respect to his written works. First, it is unclear how widely his written works were disseminated and actively used. Certain of his writings, for example his *Life of Antony*, had an enormous influence in both the East and the West, and several of his treatises and letters are cited frequently by later writers. But it appears that Athanasius was revered more than he was read. Consequently, there is no commentarial tradition on his major texts that we can track.

Second, some writings attributed to him, and by which he was best known, turn out not to have come from his pen. There is a broad pseudo-Athanasian corpus that often proved more popular than his actual writings. The most influential example is the Athanasian Creed, probably composed in late fifth-century Gaul. It functioned in the

2. See especially Socrates, *Historia ecclesiastica*, 4.20; and Theodoret, *Historia ecclesiastica*, 1.7, 4.17. For an overview and evaluation of these three church historians, see Gwynn, *Athanasius of Alexandria*, 168–70. Gwynn (*Athanasius of Alexandria*, 168) astutely observes that "the independent value of these three ecclesiastical historians for our knowledge of Athanasius is limited. For Eastern Christian tradition, their importance was immense."

3. Young, *From Nicaea to Chalcedon*, 69.

4. For Philostorgius's anti-Athanasian testimony, see Timothy D. Barnes, *Athanasius and Constantius: Theology and Politics in the Constantinian Empire* (Cambridge, MA: Harvard University Press, 1993); and Duane Wade-Hampton Arnold, *The Early Episcopal Career of Athanasius of Alexandria* (Notre Dame: University of Notre Dame Press, 1991).

Western church both as a standard of orthodoxy and as the prime representative statement of Athanasius's teaching. Athanasius's genuine writings are certainly not unimportant for his reception in the Christian tradition, but it is preeminently his perseverance in great trial and the faith he contended for, enshrined in the Nicene and Athanasian Creeds, that stand out as the principal emblems of his achievement.

The account of Athanasius's reception that follows makes no claim to thoroughness. The goal, rather, is to be representative. We will begin by examining his reception in the East, especially in the period immediately following his death, and then turn to investigate how he was received in the West, with a special focus on the role of the Athanasian Creed. We will then examine two illuminating and intriguing contra and pro Athanasius tendencies marked by the figures of Isaac Newton and John Henry Newman respectively. Finally, we will bring the account up to the present day by considering and evaluating the various contemporary—and contrasting—readings of Athanasius's teaching and character.

4

The Reception of Athanasius in the Eastern Tradition

> O holy father Athanasius, like a pillar of orthodoxy
> you refuted the heretical nonsense of Arius
> by insisting that the Father and the Son are equal in essence.
> O venerable father, beg Christ our God to save our souls.
>
> —Troparion to Athanasius[1]

The Eastern Christian tradition has received Athanasius as a champion of orthodoxy and a pillar of the church's faith. This is true of the Byzantine churches, but equally of the Maronites and the non-Chalcedonian Eastern churches (Coptic, Armenian, and Syrian churches).[2] In the words of George Dragas, Athanasius's "spiritual fame and radiance made him the spokesman of orthodoxy par excellence."[3] The issue in question is not *whether* Athanasius was well received and appreciated in the East but *how* he was received and what particular impact he had on the Eastern tradition. To examine this, we will first look at

1. "Athanasius of Alexandria," Orthodox Wiki, February 7, 2013, http://tinyurl.com/lfq5nlg.
2. For an overview of the reception of Athanasius in the various Eastern churches, see Peter Gemeinhardt, ed., *Athanasius Handbuch* (Tübingen: Mohr Siebeck, 2011), 390–420; and Gwynn, *Athanasius of Alexandria*, 184–93.
3. Dragas, *St. Athanasius of Alexandria*, 204.

the proximate reception of Athanasius in Basil of Caesarea, Gregory of Nazianzus, Cyril of Alexandria, and the early monastic movement. Then we will briefly consider two controversies in the later Byzantine tradition in which Athanasius's legacy played a role: the controversy over the use of icons and the collision with the West over the theology of the *filioque*.

Basil of Caesarea

General summaries of the fourth century often depict Athanasius and the Cappadocian fathers (Basil, Gregory of Nazianzus, and Gregory of Nyssa) as if they were runners in a relay race. As the story is told, Athanasius ran the long, hard leg of the race from the Council of Nicaea, finally handing the baton over to the three fleet-footed Cappadocians who (in turn) carried the race through to the Council of Constantinople and beyond. Though it makes too simple what is in fact a complex relationship, this rough depiction has much to commend it. According to John Behr, "While it would be too simplistic to present Basil as taking over the baton of orthodoxy from Athanasius and continuing in the path that he has thus far defined, Basil's work does in fact complement that of Athanasius remarkably well."[4] Bringing nuance to this picture, Behr goes on to say that "all of this was not so much a straightforward continuation or development of Athanasius' own defense of Nicaea, but Basil's own proper contributions, complementing that of Athanasius."[5] Speaking in a similar vein, Lewis Ayres observes that "tracing the actual influence of Athanasius on his contemporaries is difficult," and that "his influence on the Cappadocians is much more difficult to demonstrate."[6] Basil and the two Gregorys were plainly not Athanasius's direct disciples. Which of Athanasius's writings they read and what influence his writings had upon them remain open questions. Yet, from the direct testimony of Basil and Gregory of Nazianzen, it is clear that they saw themselves contending for the same faith and viewed Athanasius as a champion of the race that they were also continuing to run.

We are fortunate to possess six letters from Basil to Athanasius, and a further five that reflect Basil's view of Athanasius.[7] The focus of

4. Behr, *Nicene Faith*, part 2, 264.
5. Ibid., 265.
6. Ayres, *Nicaea and Its Legacy*, 143n30.
7. The letters from Basil to Athanasius are *Epistles* 61, 66, 67, 69, 80, 82; Basil's letters referring to Athanasius are *Ep.* 90, 154, 204, 214, 258.

nearly every letter is the so-called "Melitian schism," a division in the city of Antioch over which of two claimants was the rightful bishop. Basil favored Melitius while Athanasius backed Paulinus.[8] In 371–72, Basil sent several letters to Athanasius in the hope of persuading him to throw his considerable support behind Melitius. In one instance, praising Athanasius, Basil calls upon the aged patriarch to use his influence with the West to help unite Antioch around Melitius:

> But, to carry out these objects, who has more capacity than yourself, with your intelligence and prudence? Who is keener to see the needful course to be taken? Who has more practical experience in working a profitable policy? Who feels more deeply the troubles of the brethren? What through all the West is more honoured than your venerable gray hairs? O most honoured father, leave behind you some memorial worthy of your life and character. By this one act crown your innumerable efforts on behalf of true religion.[9]

In the end, Basil's appeal to Athanasius was not successful; the Alexandrian bishop died in 373 without bringing about a healing of the rupture in Antioch. But this did not cause Basil to lose his esteem for Athanasius. Writing (ca. 375) shortly after Athanasius's death, Basil justifies his own pastoral action according to Athanasius's counsel and example:

> For after receiving the letter of the very blessed Father Athanasius, bishop of Alexandria, which I hold in my hand, and show to anyone who asks, wherein he has distinctly declared that any one expressing a wish to come over from the heresy of the Arians and accepting the Nicene Creed, is to be received without hesitation and difficulty, citing in support of his opinion the unanimous assent of the bishops of Macedonia and of Asia; I, considering myself bound to follow the high authority of such a man and of those who made the rule, and with every desire on my own part to win the reward promised to peacemakers, did enroll in the lists of communicants all who accepted that creed.[10]

This narrow window onto the interactions of the two great figures reveals Basil's deep respect and regard for "father" Athanasius. Though

8. For details of the schism, see Hubertus R. Drobner, *The Fathers of the Church: A Comprehensive Introduction*, trans. Siegfried S. Schatzmann (Peabody, MA: Hendrickson, 2007), 202–4.
9. Basil, *Ep.* 66; in *St. Basil: Letters and Select Works, Nicene and Post-Nicene Fathers*, series 2, vol. 8, trans. Philip Schaff and Henry Wace (Edinburgh: T&T Clark, 1986), 163–64. Philip Schaff and Henry Wace, trans., *Nicene and Post-Nicene Fathers*, series 2, 14 vols. (Edinburgh: T&T Clark, 1986), hereafter referred to as *NPNF*^{2}.
10. Basil, *Ep.* 204.6; in *St. Basil*, 245.

no mention is made of points of doctrine, the tone of Basil's appeals and his imitation of Athanasius's peace-making practice makes no sense apart from a basic agreement on the essentials of the faith.

Gregory of Nazianzus

During a sojourn in the city of Constantinople in 379–80, just a half-dozen years after the death of Athanasius, Gregory of Nazianzus delivered an oration dedicated entirely to the praise of the great Athanasius. Though undoubtedly hyperbolic at points, the oration reveals Gregory's own deep appreciation for the conduct and teaching of Athanasius, and, crucially, it set the standard for how Athanasius would be regarded for generations to come.

Gregory opens by praising virtue and extolling Athanasius as one who excelled in all virtue: "In praising Athanasius, I shall be praising virtue. To speak of him and to praise virtue are identical, because he had, or, to speak more truly, has embraced virtue in its entirety."[11] Lauding Athanasius for his excellence in both intellect and activity, Nazianzen acknowledges that a full history of the great man is warranted (and that he himself hopes to compose such a history on the model of Athanasius's own *Life of Antony*), but for the present he is offering a panegyric that has space only for recounting a few historical incidents.[12]

Gregory expresses his admiration for Athanasius first of all for his knowledge of the Scriptures and the contemplative wisdom drawn from the holy writings: "From meditating on every book of the Old and New Testament, with a depth such as none else has applied even to one of them, [Athanasius] grew rich in contemplation, rich in splendour of life, combining them in wondrous sort by that golden bond which few can weave."[13] Endorsing the legitimacy of his election as bishop of Alexandria, Gregory applauds Athanasius for the balance he attained in challenging circumstances:

> He was sublime in action, lowly in mind; inaccessible in virtue, most accessible in intercourse; gentle, free from anger, sympathetic, sweet in words, sweeter in disposition; angelic in appearance, more angelic in mind; calm in rebuke, persuasive in praise, without spoiling the good effect of either by excess, but rebuking with the tenderness of a father, praising with the

11. Gregory of Nazianzus, *Or.* 21.1; in *S. Cyril of Jerusalem, S. Gregory of Nazianzus, NPNF^2*, 7:269.
12. Gregory, *Or.* 21.5; in *NPNF^2*, 7:270.
13. Gregory, *Or.* 21.6; in *NPNF^2*, 7:270–71.

> dignity of a ruler, his tenderness was not dissipated, nor his severity sour; for the one was reasonable, the other prudent, and both truly wise.[14]

Turning to doctrinal matters, Gregory commends Athanasius for holding the truths of the faith against the extremes of Arianism and Sabellianism. In contrast to the majority of bishops, whom Gregory judges to have fallen into impiety, he singles out Athanasius for his faithfulness, calling him a "pillar of the Church."[15] In a suggestive phrase, Gregory states that the emperor Julian (the Apostate) sought to overcome "Athanasius and the power of his teaching over us."[16] Gregory seems to acknowledge here the broad authority of Athanasius's teaching for the Christian people, including Gregory himself.

Twice toward the close of the oration, Gregory displays his acquaintance with Athanasius's writings. In the first, Gregory honors Athanasius, not only for defending the full divinity of the Son and holding to the Trinity, but specifically for being among the first to exposit clearly the full divinity of the Holy Spirit:

> For, when all the rest who sympathised with us were divided into three parties, and many were faltering in their conception of the Son, and still more in that of the Holy Spirit . . . and few indeed were sound upon both points, he was the first and only one, or with the concurrence of but a few, to venture to confess in writing, with entire clearness and distinctness, the unity of Godhead and essence of the three Persons, and thus to attain in later days, under the influence of inspiration, to the same faith in regard to the Holy Spirit, as had been bestowed at an earlier time on most of the Fathers in regard to the Son.[17]

Gregory here seems plainly aware of the *Letters to Serapion* in which Athanasius argues decisively for the full divinity of the Spirit. This was a matter most precious to Gregory; in his fifth and final theological oration, also given at Constantinople, he insists with great force on the full divinity of the Spirit.

In the second instance, Gregory lauds the Alexandrian for his intervention with the Antiochenes, helping them to recognize the sameness of faith in different formulations. To make the following statement, Gregory must have been acquainted with Athanasius's *Tome to the Antiochenes* (written in 362):

14. Gregory, *Or*. 21.9; in *NPNF*², 7:271–72.
15. Gregory, *Or*. 21.26; in *NPNF*², 7:276.
16. Gregory, *Or*. 21.32; in *NPNF*², 7:279.
17. Gregory, *Or*. 21.33; in *NPNF*², 7:279, modified.

> Seeing and hearing this, our blessed one, true man of God and great steward of souls as he was, felt it inconsistent with his duty to overlook so absurd and unreasonable a rending of the word, and applied his medicine to the disease. In what manner? He conferred in his gentle and sympathetic way with both parties, and after he had carefully weighed the meaning of their expressions, and found that they had the same sense, and were in nowise different in doctrine, by permitting each party to use its own terms, he bound them together in unity of action.[18]

Concluding the oration in a paean of praise for Athanasius, Gregory declares that "his life and habits form the ideal of an Episcopate, and his teaching the law of orthodoxy."[19]

In sum, Gregory defends Athanasius against the charges of his calumniators and presents him as a bishop of excelling virtue. He approves his teaching, showing some acquaintance with Athanasius's writings, but even more he praises him for his conduct, presenting him as a model of the servant of God. This "Gregorian portrait" of Athanasius would become the standard version handed down in the Christian tradition.[20]

Cyril of Alexandria

Both in the Christian tradition and in contemporary scholarship, Athanasius and Cyril of Alexandria are bound firmly together. Cyril is commonly seen as the true heir of Athanasius in doctrine, ecclesiology, and pragmatic church politics. Whether praised or excoriated, the two are inextricably joined, with Cyril viewed as the extension (and development) of Athanasius. There are, however, two distinct and divergent narratives, each one having ancient and modern advocates. The first narrative acclaims Athanasius and Cyril as great figures who stood firm against a serious doctrinal deviation; by their orthodox teaching and unflagging perseverance, they helped the church reach and maintain doctrinal clarity on the full divinity and humanity of the one

18. Gregory, *Or.* 21.35; in *NPNF*², 7:279. Christopher A. Beeley (*Gregory of Nazianzus on the Trinity and the Knowledge of God: In Your Light We Shall See Light* [New York: Oxford University Press, 2008], 279), judges that Gregory probably had direct acquaintance with only two of Athanasius's works (*Life of Antony* and *Letter to Jovinian*). Based on Gregory's testimony here, however, it appears that he knew of at least two other writings (*Letters to Serapion* and *Tome to the Antiochenes*). Gwynn (*Athanasius of Alexandria*, 14) also concludes that both Basil and Nazianzen very probably had direct access to the *Letters to Serapion*.
19. Gregory, *Or.* 21.37; in *NPNF*², 7:280.
20. Jerome notably indicates his knowledge of Gregory's oration to Athanasius in his *De viris illustribus*, 117.

Son (Trinity and Christology). On this view, Cyril is Athanasius's heir both in the excellence of his teaching and in the firmness of his character. This is fundamentally the picture that Nazianzen paints of Athanasius.[21]

The second narrative, one sharply critical of both figures, judges Athanasius's teaching to be theologically unsophisticated and doctrinally flawed. Cyril repeats and re-presents this teaching, with flaws embedded, adding little or nothing of his own. Athanasius is the defective innovator; Cyril dutifully and uncritically plods behind in steps already laid out before him. Pastorally, this second narrative depicts Athanasius as the original "gangster-style" Alexandrian bishop whom Cyril imitated with precision and alacrity, outdoing his master in shrewd political maneuvering. Together, they serve as prime exemplars of the abusive, deceitful prelate who uses doctrine as a weapon for personal power and who rides roughshod over any who stand in his way.[22]

Here, we will examine how Cyril of Alexandria received, applied, and developed Athanasius's legacy, reserving a broader estimation of Athanasius's teaching and character for the final chapter. One significant impediment we face is that Cyril almost never cites authorities that he freely uses. He names a source only when that author is beneficial for presenting his case—when, for example, he calls upon Athanasius, Basil, and others and quotes from specific texts—to undergird his christological teaching against the Antiochenes. By examining the few occasions when Cyril refers to Athanasius by name, we will obtain a basic understanding of how he viewed his predecessor; by tracking Cyril's anonymous use of Athanasius's writings, we can hope to grasp the basic contours of Cyril's theological relationship to Athanasius.

One rare pre-Nestorian mention of Athanasius in Cyril's writings appears in his *Festal Letter* for the year 420. Cyril is describing the incarnation of the Word, seeking to explain the conjunction of the Word with his "flesh." He insists that the phrase, "the Word became flesh" (John 1:14), does not mean that the Word changed into flesh but that the Word united the whole of humanity to himself in an indescribable union. At this juncture, he calls upon the testimony of Athanasius to

21. Contemporary versions of this positive narrative can be found, for example, in Michael E. Molloy, *Champion of Truth: The Life of Saint Athanasius* (New York: Society of St. Paul, 2003); and Jack N. Sparks, *The Resurrection Letters* (Nashville: Thomas Nelson, 1979).

22. Contemporary versions of this critical narrative appear in R. P. C. Hanson, *The Search for the Christian Doctrine of God: The Arian Controversy 318-381* (Edinburgh: T&T Clark, 1988); and Barnes, *Athanasius and Constantius*.

support his claim, referring not to a specific text but to the teaching of Athanasius on this point as found generally in his writings:

> Surely, then, as our all-praiseworthy father and bishop Athanasius, the undistorted rule of the orthodox faith, has said as well in his own writings, what has happened is a conjunction in the same place of two realities by nature dissimilar, divinity and humanity. But there is one Christ from the two.[23]

Cyril's appeal to Athanasius as "the undistorted rule of the orthodox faith" shows the high level of authority that Cyril grants to Athanasius and anticipates how Cyril will appeal to Athanasius in the wake of the Nestorian controversy.

Direct appeals to Athanasius multiply when Cyril comes under attack from the Antiochene theologians and must defend himself against charges that his teaching is novel and unsound. One of the earliest anti-Nestorian works, *Letter to the Monks of Egypt* (429), provides a true paean to Athanasius. Cyril calls upon the testimony of his predecessor to show the orthodoxy and ancestry of the term *Theotokos* for Mary:

> We have been taught to think this way by the holy Fathers. Our Father Athanasius, of illustrious memory, was an ornament to the throne of the church of Alexandria throughout forty-six years in all. He opposed an unconquered and apostolic wisdom to the sophistries of the evil heretics, and refreshed the whole world with his own writings as if they were some most fragrant balsam. His orthodoxy and godliness in teaching are confessed by all, and he composed a book for us concerning the holy and consubstantial Trinity where, throughout the third discourse, he calls the holy virgin the Mother of God. I will make use of his own sayings and the exact words are these.[24]

Whether or not Cyril knew of Gregory's oration in honor of Athanasius, his praise of the patriarch here resembles that longer work, underlining both the unimpeachable orthodoxy of Athanasius's teaching and the godliness of his conduct. When in other post-Nestorian letters Cyril makes direct appeal to Athanasius's authority, he generally quotes from the *Treatises Against the Arians* or the *Letter to Epictetus*.[25]

23. Cyril, *Festal Letter*, 8.6; in Cyril of Alexandria, *Festal Letters 1–12*, trans. Philip R. Amidon, ed. John J. O'Keefe, Fathers of the Church 118 (Washington, DC: Catholic University of America Press: 2009), 149–50.
24. Cyril, *Letter to the Monks of Egypt*, 6; translated in *St. Cyril of Alexandria and the Christological Controversy*, by John McGuckin (Crestwood, NY: St. Vladimir's Seminary Press, 2004), 247.

Among scholars, no one doubts that Cyril saw himself as promoting the teaching—the theological "program"—of Athanasius. Norman Russell estimates that Athanasius was "the greatest influence on [Cyril's] theological development."[26] Searching for sources of Cyril's theology, Lionel Wickham draws the same conclusion: Cyril's "clearest debt is to Athanasius."[27] The question is how to view the relation between the two figures. Is Cyril simply parroting the teaching of Athanasius or is there genuine development? If there is development, where is it to be found?

Cyril most clearly follows in the steps of Athanasius when teaching on the divinity of the Son and the Trinitarian reality of God. One of his earliest works, the *Thesaurus*, is largely a digest of Athanasius's *Discourses Against the Arians*.[28] In her magisterial work on Cyril's Trinitarian doctrine, Marie-Odile Boulnois agrees that Cyril follows in the path forged by Athanasius and so "remains fundamentally Alexandrian," but she concludes that Cyril, drawing on the technical language of the Cappadocians, elaborates his own unique synthesis. His primary accomplishment is a more richly developed theology of the Holy Spirit.[29] Brian Daley concurs, arguing that Cyril is not just derivative of Athanasius and Didymus, as many scholars assume. Rather, Cyril presents a synthesis of Athanasius and the Cappadocians with "its own characteristic emphases and themes."[30]

What about the topic of Christology? Does Cyril follow the incarnational soteriology that Athanasius forged? John O'Keefe believes that he does: "The basic contours of Cyril's Christology follow the same pattern as that established by Athanasius and are determined by his

25. Cyril provides a full citation from both works in *A Defense of the Twelve Anathemas against the Bishops of the Diocese of Oriens*; see Cyril of Alexandria, *Three Christological Treatises*, trans. Daniel King, Fathers of the Church 129 (Washington, DC: Catholic University of America Press, 2014), 137. On several occasions, Cyril tells his readers that his opponents have circulated a doctored edition of Athanasius's *Letter to Epictetus*, making false interpolations to accord with their teaching. In response, Cyril promises to send an accurate copy of the letter so that all can see what Athanasius actually wrote. See Cyril, *Ep.* 39.11 (to John of Antioch); Cyril, *Ep.* 45.11 (first Letter to Succensus); Cyril, *Ep.* 40.21 (to Acacius); and Cyril, *Ep.* 67.7 (to John of Antioch).

26. Norman Russell, *Cyril of Alexandria* (London: Routledge, 2000), 206n18.

27. Lionel Wickham, introduction to *Cyril of Alexandria: Select Letters*, ed. and trans. Lionel Wickham (Oxford: Clarendon, 1983), xv.

28. Ibid.

29. Marie-Odile Boulnois, *Le paradoxe trinitaire chez Cyrille d'Alexandrie* (Paris: Institut des Études Augustiniennes, 1994), 595, 597.

30. Brian Daley, "The Fullness of the Saving God: Cyril of Alexandria on the Holy Spirit," in *The Theology of Cyril of Alexandria: A Critical Appreciation*, ed. Thomas G. Weinandy and Daniel A. Keating (London: T&T Clark, 2003), 115. Frances Young (*From Nicaea to Chalcedon*, 308) offers a similar estimation of Cyril's teaching on the Trinity: "Athanasius' ideas are used but they are reordered and given totally new expression so as to present a more rigorous form of argument."

soteriological vision. Christ is the Son of God, the second person of the Trinity, understood in a thoroughly Nicene framework."[31] Khaled Anatolios reckons that Cyril "based his own Christological reflections in large part along the lines of his predecessor."[32] Obviously, Cyril is well downstream from Athanasius when the crisis surrounding Nestorius breaks in 429. New issues have appeared and new arguments are required. Cyril appeals repeatedly to Athanasius's *Letter to Epictetus* as the foundation for his own teaching about Christ, but he does not simply repeat what Athanasius had said. He makes use of other sources as well, notably Gregory of Nazianzus's *Letters to Cledonius*, but always puts his own distinct stamp on his teaching. Cyril is not simply a compiler of opinions; he readily draws upon many sources, Athanasius being the principle one, to compose a theological statement that is fully his own.

The doctrine of deification offers a further example of how Cyril follows Athanasius closely yet brings his own distinctive approach to bear. According to Norman Russell, Cyril follows Athanasius in viewing the incarnation of the Word as the ground for human deification. For both figures, "the deification (*theopoiēsis*) of the flesh by the Word makes possible the deification of the individual believer through a personal participation in Christ."[33] Yet, Russell judges that Cyril's teaching on deification "represents a considerable advance on Athanasius" by virtue of its relation to the entire Trinity, its richer theological anthropology, and its inclusion of the Eucharist in the activity of deification.[34] Though Cyril largely eschews the technical terminology of deification found abundantly in Athanasius, he enriches the doctrine itself.

Christopher Beeley has questioned whether Cyril's achievements in Christology are really a reception of Athanasius at all.[35] He puts forward Nazianzen as the dominant source of Cyril's best christological insights; Cyril's dependence on Athanasius only bleeds through when he fails to fully integrate Gregory's profound insights. In short, where Cyril's Christology shines it is due to Nazianzen; where it limps, the lingering influence of Athanasius can still be seen. Beeley is certainly warranted in claiming Gregory as a significant source for

31. John O'Keefe, introduction to Cyril, *Festal Letters 1–12*, 27.
32. Khaled Anatolios, *Athanasius* (London: Routledge, 2004), 33.
33. Russell, *Cyril of Alexandria*, 235n44.
34. Norman Russell, *The Doctrine of Deification in the Greek Patristic Tradition* (Oxford: Oxford University Press, 2004), 192.
35. Christopher A. Beeley, "Cyril of Alexandria and Gregory Nazianzen: Tradition and Complexity in Patristic Christology," *Journal of Early Christian Studies* 17, no. 3 (2009): 381–419. Beeley re-proposes this argument in a subsequent study: *The Unity of Christ: Continuity and Conflict in Patristic Tradition* (New Haven: Yale University Press, 2012), 257–72.

Cyril's christological teaching, but the wedge that he seeks to create between the teaching of Athanasius and Cyril is unpersuasive. Beeley paints Cyril as rising above Athanasius's dualistic Christology (due to Nazianzen's benevolent influence): "Cyril's happy embrace of divine suffering overruled Athanasius's opposition to it." But he then bemoans Cyril's failure to maintain this commitment throughout his corpus to divine suffering because of Cyril's "lingering discomfort with theopaschite language," causing him to "abandon Gregory's radical affirmation of God's suffering in Christ."[36] But this is a serious misreading of Cyril. Throughout his writings, from beginning to end, Cyril could not be clearer in stating that the eternal Son and Word genuinely suffered, but only and always as "man" (*anthropos*), never as God in his divine nature. In this he follows Athanasius closely. Moreover, Beeley's parsing of Cyril's writings (for example, the *Third Letter to Nestorius*) according to a complicated dialectic of praiseworthy Gregorian elements and inferior Athanasian influences fails to persuade.[37]

When one reads the texts of both Athanasius and Cyril together, the profound resonances and similarities become evident. Cyril plainly read Athanasius thoroughly and absorbed his thought deeply. Cyril's reception of Athanasius is a matter not of adopting select passages or stray ideas here and there but of taking on an entire way of thinking about the divine economy and the place of Christ within it. As contemporary scholarship has recognized, however, Cyril is a profound theologian in his own right. The influence of many others besides Athanasius, Gregory of Nazianzen being one of them, contribute to this depth. But arguably the single greatest source for Cyril's synthesis derives not from any of his predecessors but from his own close attention to the Bible, displayed in his massive commentaries on nearly the entirety of the Old and New Testaments.

Athanasius and the Early Monastic Movement

Even Athanasius's severest critics acknowledge that he forged an effective alliance with the monks of Egypt and became their trusted ally and leader. Perhaps the greatest element of Athanasius's legacy—and certainly the one for which he is most beloved—is his lasting impact on the monastic movement and the ascetic life.[38] The chief vehicle was his *Life*

36. See Beeley, *Unity in Christ*, 167, 271, 269.
37. For Beeley's complicated parsing of sources, see Beeley, "Cyril of Alexandria," 413–15; Beeley, *Unity of Christ*, 269.

of Antony, a work that within Athanasius's own lifetime became standard reading and soon after his death enjoyed wide dissemination in both the East and West. But Athanasius also formed bonds of friendship and loyalty with the monastic communities of his day, achieving a cooperative relationship between the episcopate and the desert that would come to mark his successors, Theophilus and Cyril.

Gregory of Nazianzen praises Athanasius for both these accomplishments. Gregory notes that Athanasius "wrote the life of the divine Antony, and set forth, in the form of a narrative, the laws of the monastic life."[39] Gregory shrewdly perceives that in *The Life of Antony*, Athanasius did not merely compose an edifying biography but laid down the fundamental principles of the ascetic vocation. The impact of this *Life* on the ascetic imagination is incalculable. On the other hand, in Gregory's eyes, Athanasius succeeded in bringing together the solitary and communal manifestations of monastic life, as well as the active and contemplative expressions of Christian spirituality:

> During his intercourse with [the monks], the great Athanasius, who was always the mediator and reconciler of all other men . . . reconciled the solitary with the community life: by showing that the priesthood is capable of contemplation, and that contemplation is in need of a spiritual guide. Thus he combined the two, and so united the partisans of both calm action and of active calm.[40]

In a study on Athanasius's interaction with the ascetic movement, David Brakke investigates how Athanasius's political and theological aims guided his relationship with the monks.[41] Brakke proposes that "the Athanasian Antony is not first of all a patron, a teacher, or a party leader: he is simply the ideal Christian, the most dramatic example of someone who, thanks to Christ's victory on the cross, is making his journey on the way up to heaven."[42] He recognizes that "Athanasius hopes to contribute to the formation of a Christian *politeia* by fostering an ethic of imitation that reflects his own programme of self-formation through imitation of the saints."[43] Yet Brakke's lens for viewing *The Life of Antony* and Athanasius's relationship with the monks is a political

38. Gwynn, (*Athanasius of Alexandria*, 178–79, 192) concludes that for both the Western and Coptic traditions, Athanasius is most highly prized for the ideal of the monastic life that he framed.
39. Gregory, *Or.* 21.5; in *NPNF*^{2}, 7:270.
40. Gregory, *Or.* 21.19–20; in *NPNF*^{2}, 7:274–75.
41. Brakke, *Athanasius.*
42. Ibid., 216.
43. Ibid., 245.

one; he seeks to offer "a more precise understanding of how asceticism advanced Athanasius' political programme."[44]

Athanasius was undoubtedly tactical in how he courted relationship with the monastic communities, but his expressed appreciation for the ascetic life would seem to be more than just politically instrumental. In the words of David Gwynn, "Whether it is correct to speak of the 'politics' of asceticism is more open to debate. . . . To dismiss Athanasius' alliance with the monks and virgins of Alexandria and Egypt as merely political manipulation is to do Athanasius and the ascetics alike a grave disservice."[45] Further, Brakke's claim that "Athanasius removed intellectual contemplation of God from the centre of his spirituality, and instead defined the Christian life in ascetic terms as control of the body's passions and cultivation of virtue" is one-sided.[46] The *Letter to Marcellinus on the Psalms* and the widely disseminated work *On the Incarnation* offer outlines of a spirituality where intellectual contemplation of God finds a secure home.

The Reception of Athanasius in the Byzantine Tradition

Athanasius is a figure of great renown in the Byzantine tradition. He is named as an authority in three ecumenical councils (Constantinople II and III, Nicaea II) and was the subject of multiple panegyrics in the Byzantine period.[47] Frank L. Cross traces the wider dissemination of his writings in the East to the mid-fifth century and concludes that "the manuscript tradition leaves little doubt that from the first they were divided into two main groups, the Apologetic and the Doctrinal Treatises."[48] How broadly Athanasius's works were known and read in the East is difficult to assess with precision. We have evidence for the wide flourishing of *The Life of Antony*. John Behr also identifies *On the Incarnation* as a deeply influential work: "*On the Incarnation*, in particular, had a massive impact on later theology. It could almost be described as the defining exposition of Nicene theology, certainly as understood by the later Byzantine tradition."[49] Among the doctrinal works, the *Orations Against the Arians* and the *Letter to Epictetus* figure prominently, but the *Letters to Serapion* and *Tome to the Antiochenes* also have echoes in

44. Ibid., 14.
45. Gwynn, *Athanasius of Alexandria*, 120.
46. Brakke, *Athanasius*, 144.
47. See Gemeinhardt, *Athanasius Handbuch*, 416.
48. Frank L. Cross, *The Study of St. Athanasius* (Oxford: Clarendon, 1945), 6.
49. Behr, *Nicene Faith*, part 1, 168–69.

later writers. Athanasius's apologetic works (for example, *Defense of His Flight*) were read and digested by Socrates, Sozomen, and Theodoret. Whether through Athanasius's own words or those of his advocates, the details of his life filtered down through the tradition. Within this broad and positive reception of Athanasius in the East, we will briefly consider two contexts in which Athanasius's legacy played a notable part: the iconoclastic controversy and the *filioque* controversy.[50]

The Iconoclastic Controversy

The debate over the use of icons in the Eastern church broke into the open in the late 720s. The issue in question was whether the making and veneration of icons (pictures of Christ, Mary, the angels, and the saints) is a praiseworthy act or whether it violates the commandment against the making of graven images. The Byzantine emperor, Leo II, vigorously championed the anti-icon position; opposing him, many bishops and monks took a stand in favor of the veneration of icons—among them was John of Damascus. Writing in the late 730s and early 740s from Palestine under the rule of the Muslim caliph, John undertook a theological defense of the veneration of icons, providing a needed clarification of what veneration was and how the act of venerating icons not only did not violate God's command but was positively expressive of the reality of the incarnation.

John makes reference to the testimony of Athanasius four times in his compendium of theology, *On the Orthodox Faith*, calling him "the blessed Athanasius," "holy Athanasius," "the divine Athanasius," and "the renowned Athanasius."[51] He refers to Athanasius (and Cyril) favorably when speaking about how the divinity was united to the flesh in Christ in the incarnation, and he appeals to Athanasius's *Letters to Serapion*, adopting Athanasius's form of argumentation to show that the Holy Spirit is not among created beings.[52] All this shows Damascene's wider reliance on Athanasius's thought. But notably, in his *Third Apology*, John makes a creative use of a selection from Athanasius's third *Oration Against the Arians* (3.5) to undergird the practice of the veneration of icons. In the text John cites, Athanasius holds up the example

50. I am indebted to Norman Russell for drawing my attention to the significant role Athanasius played in the iconoclastic and *filioque* controversies.

51. John of Damascus, *De fide orthodoxa*, 3.6, 10, 16, 23; 4.6; in *St. John of Damascus: Writings*, trans. Frederic H. Chase, Fathers of the Church 37 (Washington, DC: Catholic University of America Press, 1958), 281, 288, 314, 341.

52. John of Damascus, *De fide orth.*, 3.6, 3.16.

of the emperor and his image to show how the worship of the image is equivalent to the worship of the one who is imaged.

> If we use the example of the emperor's image we will find this easier to understand. The image bears his form and appearance. Whatever the emperor looks like, that is how his image appears. The likeness of the emperor on the image is precisely similar to the emperor's own appearance, so that anyone who looks at the image recognizes that it is the emperor's image; also, anyone who sees the emperor first and image later, realizes at once whose image it is. Since the likenesses are interchangeable, the image might answer someone who wished to see the emperor after he had seen the image, "The emperor and I are one, for I am in him, and he is in me. That which you see in me you will also see in him, and if you should see him, you will recognize us to be the same." He who venerates the image venerates the emperor depicted on it, for the image is his form and his likeness.[53]

This is a fascinating reminting of an analogy drawn from worship of the emperor's image. In the original context, Athanasius employs this example to show that worship of the Son, who is the image of God, is worship directed to the Father, so there is but one worship of both Father and Son. The image in this case is a *person*—the incarnate Word of God—who is rightly worshiped along with the Father. In the later context, John extends the analogy to apply to the written or painted image (icon) of Christ. In this case, the image acts as a window to what it images, and the veneration offered to the image is directed to the one who is imaged (in this case Christ).

This use of Athanasius's teaching to speak to the question of the veneration of icons was replicated by later authorities. The Seventh Ecumenical Council, held at Nicaea in 787, cites in its fourth session the same passage from Athanasius as part of the testimony from the fathers in favor of the veneration of icons.[54] Then, in the midst of a second outbreak of iconoclastic activity in the next century, Theodore the Studite calls upon this same text in Athanasius to justify the veneration of images.[55] Though Athanasius probably did not have the veneration of icons in view when he composed this text against the Arians of his

53. John of Damascus, *On the Divine Images: Three Apologies Against Those Who Attack the Divine Images*, trans. David Anderson (Crestwood, NY: St. Vladimir's Seminary Press, 1980), 101.

54. John Mendham, trans., *The Seventh General Council, the Second of Nicaea: In Which the Worship of Images Was Established* (London: W. E. Painter, 1849), 196.

55. Theodore the Studite, *On the Holy Icons*, 2.13; in *On the Holy Icons*, trans. Catharine P. Roth (Crestwood, NY: St. Vladimir's Seminary Press, 2001), 49–50.

day, the later tradition extended its application in a way unforeseen but consistent with the theological trajectory of Athanasius's thought.

The *Filioque* Controversy

The Latin addition of "and the Son" (*filioque*) to the Nicene Creed engendered a running dialogue, debate, and disagreement between the East and West that continues even today. As early as the seventh century, Maximus the Confessor, an Eastern father, became aware of this addition and the theology behind it. In his *Letter to Marinus*, he describes what the Latins mean by the addition and seeks to explain the *filioque* in a way consistent with the Greek approach that sees the Father as the cause of the Spirit's procession. This conciliatory approach, one that makes allowances for differences in language, does not generally characterize either side in the debates that followed.

Athanasius first appears as a witness in a dialogue held between Greek and Latin representatives meeting at Nicaea in 1234. Both Athanasius and Cyril were cited by the Western participants in support of the *filioque*, but no texts from Athanasius are named and no agreements were reached.[56] Writing around the same time period, Thomas Aquinas cites the authority of Athanasius to settle the question of whether the Spirit proceeds from the Father and the Son: "On the contrary, Athanasius says: 'The Holy Spirit is from the Father and the Son; not made, nor created, nor begotten, but proceeding.'"[57] But Thomas is quoting from verse 23 of the Athanasian Creed, a creed not recognized by the East and not, in fact, composed by Athanasius.

At the Council of Ferrara-Florence in 1438–39, called in large part to bring about a reunion of East and West, Athanasius reappears as a key witness for the Western side of the debate. At the fifth session in Ferrara (October 1438), the Latin side brought forward a collection of patristic texts from both Eastern and Western fathers in support of the procession of the Spirit from the Father and the Son. Included in this catena was a reference to Athanasius's *First Epistle to Serapion*. After the council moved to Florence, the debate was resumed in March of 1439 during the third and fourth sessions, and this same text from Athanasius again became a point of contention.[58] It reads: "But if, in regard to

56. See Henry Chadwick, *East and West: The Making of a Rift in the Church: From Apostolic Times until the Council of Florence* (Oxford: Oxford University Press, 2003), 238–42.
57. Thomas Aquinas, *Summa Theologiae*, 1.36.2.7; in *The "Summa Theologica" of St. Thomas Aquinas*, part 1, trans. Fathers of the Dominican Province, 2nd rev. ed., vol. 1 (London: Burns, Oates & Washbourne, 1920), http://tinyurl.com/lco8ktd.

order and nature, the Spirit bears the same relation to the Son as the Son to the Father, will not he who calls the Spirit a creature necessarily hold the same to be true of the Son?"[59] Representing the Latins, John Montenero argued that Athanasius taught an order within the Trinity that effectively contains the teaching on the *filioque*. If the Spirit is dependent on the Son just as the Son is on the Father, then the Son has a role in the procession of the Spirit. Mark Eugenicus, responding for the Greek cohort, maintained that Athanasius's purpose in this text (and in the entire work) was not to stress the distinctions in the Holy Trinity but to show that by the unity of will and operation we can see that all three persons are fully divine. On the Greek reading, Athanasius intends to say nothing more than that the Holy Spirit is conjoined and connatural with the Son.[60]

In the following session of the council, the Latins brought forward a further Athanasian text that also appears in the *First Letter to Serapion*, coming directly before the one cited above.

> As the Son, the living Word, is one, so must the vital activity and gift whereby he sanctifies and enlightens be one, perfect and complete; which is said to proceed from the Father, because it is *from the Word*, who is confessed to be from the Father, that it shines forth and is sent and is given.[61]

In this text, Athanasius speaks of the Spirit coming *from* the Son, thus demonstrating for the Western party that "from" implies origin in the proper sense.[62] The debate went forward, each side citing patristic authorities to buttress their position. Though the Athanasian Creed was included in the council documents that marked the union of the Catholic Church with the Armenian Church in November of 1439, it does not appear in the agreement with the Eastern Orthodox Church and does not seem to have arisen in the debates on the procession of the Spirit earlier that year. In the end, the agreements reached at Florence between Catholics and the Eastern churches were not sustained. The *filioque* remains a point of contention up to the present day, and Athanasius continues to be cited as teaching a view of the Spirit's procession that at least provides a bridge between the standard theologies of the East and the West.

58. Joseph Gill, *The Council of Florence* (Cambridge: Cambridge University Press, 1959), 152.
59. Athanasius, *Ad Serapionem*, 1.21; in *Letters of Saint Athanasius*, 118.
60. Gill, *Council of Florence*, 202–3.
61. Athanasius, *Ad Serapionem*, 1.20; in *Letters of Saint Athanasius*, 116–17.
62. Gill, *Council of Florence*, 218–19.

5

The Reception of Athanasius in the Western Tradition

> Later generations of Latin Christianity, like their counterparts in the Greek East, remembered Athanasius as the heroic champion of orthodoxy and as a propagator of asceticism.[1]
>
> —David Gwynn

As in the East, Athanasius was received in the West with great enthusiasm as the champion of Nicene orthodoxy. In both conduct and teaching, he stood as the exemplar of the faithful bishop and servant of God.[2] Building upon a longstanding medieval tradition, in 1568 Pope Pius V declared Athanasius—along with Basil, Gregory of Nazianzen, and John Chrysostom—one of the four great Eastern doctors of the church.

Two features characterize the Western reception of Athanasius: his texts were not as widely known in the West as they were in the East, and he was best known for a text transmitted in his name that he did not author. David Gwynn sums up the situation:

> To a greater degree than in the east . . . the western memory of Athanasius

1. Gwynn, *Athanasius of Alexandria*, 173.
2. For Athanasius's reception in the West as saint and hero, see Gemeinhardt, *Athanasius Handbuch*, 431–33.

> became increasingly separated from the bishop's original writings and historical context. Relatively few of Athanasius' Greek works were widely read or translated into Latin. . . . It is therefore unsurprising that throughout the Middle Ages Athanasius would be best known in the west for a creed that he did not write.[3]

Frank Cross concurs, pointing to the few genuine texts translated and known in the West up to the end of the middle ages:

> In the West, however, apart from the *Vita Antonii* in its almost contemporary translation by Evagrius, St. Athanasius's writings were little esteemed in the Middle Ages. It would seem that few, if any, of his treatises were translated until a quite late date, and that the references to his genuine works which occur in St. Thomas Aquinas were derived ultimately from Greek *catenae*.[4]

We will begin the account of the Western reception of Athanasius by gathering up testimony from the Latin fathers of the fourth and fifth centuries. These give an indication of how Athanasius was perceived by the great teachers and authorities in the West shortly after his death. Then we will turn to an examination of the Athanasian Creed: its origin, content, and compatibility with the teaching of Athanasius. Finally, we will briefly consider Athanasius's reception among the Reformers of the sixteenth century as a platform for the later controversies over Athanasius's legacy in the West.

Athanasius in the Western Fathers

The major Western fathers of the late fourth and early fifth centuries—Hilary, Ambrose, Jerome, Augustine, and Leo the Great—all acknowledge Athanasius by name and express appreciation for his life and teaching in a variety of ways. Hilary of Poitiers (d. ca. 368), like Basil the Great, was a contemporary of Athanasius. He has been given the epithet "Athanasius of the West" because of his defense of the Nicene faith, expressed in the twelve-book work *De Trinitate*, and "his career does bear a certain resemblance to that of the Alexandrian."[5]

3. Gwynn, *Athanasius of Alexandria*, 173.
4. Cross, *Study of St. Athanasius*, 6. Other genuine Athanasian works available in Latin translation by the early Middle Ages include: *Letter to the Monks of Egypt*, *Letter to Epictetus*, *Letter to the African Bishops*, *Letter to Adelphius*, and *Letter to Maximus*. Thomas Aquinas's *Contra errores Graecorum* also shows a more detailed knowledge of the *Letters to Serapion*. For a compilation of the genuine texts of Athanasius available to the West in the Middle Ages, see Gemeinhardt, *Athanasius Handbuch*, 378–83, 421–23.

In a work composed in 356, the first year of his exile in the Eastern empire, Hilary testifies directly to Athanasius's faithfulness in defense of the Creed of Nicaea: "Holding fast to truth he had vanquished the Arian plague in the whole of Egypt and when witnesses conspired against him on that account, a false set of charges was prepared."[6] But despite this admiration for Athanasius, Hilary never cites him or refers to him in the *De Trinitate*, and scholars tend to align his theology more closely with Basil than with Athanasius. David Gwynn sums up Hilary's relationship to Athanasius as a paradigm for the Western tradition's reception of the great Alexandrian: "Hilary's writings set a pattern for Athanasius' legacy in the West, admiration for the Alexandrian's defence of Nicaea but little detailed knowledge of this thought and writings."[7]

Ambrose, an avid reader of Greek, probably had most direct contact with Athanasius's writings of all the Western fathers and seems to draw upon them directly for his treatise on virginity and his anti-Arian work, *De Fide*.[8] Jerome refers to Athanasius on several occasions, mostly in a general way having to do with his faithfulness to the truth, to his flights, and especially to his connection with St. Antony of the Desert.[9] In a letter to Laeta instructing her on the details of her daughter's education, Jerome commends all the works of Athanasius for reading, along with those of Cyprian and Hilary of Poitiers.[10] Notably, Athanasius finds a place in Jerome's *Lives of Illustrious Men* (written after 393). In that account, Jerome supplies a list of the writings of Athanasius then currently in circulation:

> Athanasius bishop of Alexandria, hard pressed by the wiles of the Arians, fled to Constans emperor of Gaul. Returning thence with letters and, after the death of the emperor, again taking refuge in flight, he kept in hiding until the accession of Jovian, when he returned to the church and died in the reign of Valens. Various works by him are in circulation; two books *Against the nations*, one *Against Valens and Ursacius*, *On virginity*, very many *On the persecutions of the Arians*, also *On the titles of the Psalms* and *Life of Anthony the monk*, also *Festal epistles* and other works too numerous to mention."[11]

5. Gwynn, *Athanasius of Alexandria*, 174.
6. Hilary, *Against Valens and Ursacius*, 1.9.6; cited in Gwynn, *Athanasius of Alexandria*, 174.
7. Gwynn, *Athanasius of Alexandria*, 75.
8. Ibid.
9. See, e.g., Jerome, *Ep*. 68.2; Jerome, *De viris illustribus*, 88.
10. Jerome, *Ep*. 107.12.
11. Jerome, *De viris illustribus*, 87; in *Theodoret, Jerome, Gennadius, Rufinus*, *NPNF*^{2}, 3:379.

Though we could wish Jerome had filled in this list in greater detail, he gives evidence that numerous of Athanasius's works were circulating at the end of the fourth century, at least in the East where Jerome was living.

The few references to Athanasius in Augustine's vast corpus show his basic awareness of Athanasius's career, flights, and stout defense of the faith.[12] Augustine also acknowledges reading Athanasius directly but does not name specific works.[13] In a fleeting but intriguing reference in the *Confessions*, Augustine conveys Athanasius's advice on how to sing the psalms with simplicity, possibly indicating some knowledge of Athanasius's *Letter to Marcellinus on the Psalms*.[14] But according to David Gwynn, it was Augustine's encounter with Athanasius's *Life of Antony*, recounted in the *Confessions*,[15] that had the greatest impact on Augustine: "It is no small tribute to the legacy of Athanasius that this work played such a role in the formation of one of the leading minds of Latin Christianity."[16]

From Leo the Great we possess just one reference to Athanasius. In a letter written to Julian of Cos in 452, Leo informs Julian that he is sending him a copy of Athanasius's *Letter to Epictetus*, because "in it [Athanasius] has explained the Incarnation of the Word so clearly and carefully that he already beat down both Nestorius and Eutyches by anticipation in the heresies of those times. Let the followers of Eutyches and Dioscorus dare to accuse this man of such great authority of either ignorance or heresy."[17] Leo finds ample support in Athanasius for his own teaching on the full humanity and divinity of Christ.

The testimony of these Western fathers displays a basic knowledge of Athanasius's life, a deep appreciation for his witness and teaching, and a recognition of his unquestioned authority in matters of faith. Evidence for knowledge of his written works varies; several of his works are referenced and he is claimed on occasion as an authority, but perhaps only in Ambrose does Athanasius serve as a primary theological source. For them all, Athanasius functions as the undoubted touchstone of orthodoxy, but he does not function as a primary theological well from which they drink. What is conspicuously absent from

12. See, e.g., Augustine, *Ep.* 44.3.6; 148.2.10; 228.6, 10.
13. Augustine, *Ep.* 148.2.14.
14. Augustine, *Confessionum libri XIII*, 10.33.50.
15. Augustine, *Conf.*, 13.6.15.
16. Gwynn, *Athanasius of Alexandria*, 181.
17. Leo the Great, *Ep.* 109; in *St. Leo the Great: Letters*, trans. Edmund Hunt, Fathers of the Church 34 (Washington, DC: Catholic University of America Press, 1957), 195–96.

these Western writers (up to 450 CE) is any reference to the Athanasian Creed, for the simple reason that it had not yet been composed.

The Athanasian Creed

The Athanasian Creed, also known as the *Quicunque vult* (from its opening words), served as the primary written testimony to Athanasius in the West. For more than a thousand years this eloquent confession, alongside the *Life of Antony*, was the dominant written work through which Western Christians believed they heard the voice of Athanasius.[18] *The Life of Antony* communicated the spiritual teaching of the Egyptian desert; the Athanasian Creed conveyed authoritative teaching on the Trinity and the incarnation.[19] As David Gwynn maintains, "it is a document of fundamental importance to the Western legacy of Athanasius."[20]

The Creed first appears in the extant sources in the writings of Caesarius of Arles, whose tenure as bishop ran from 502 to 542. In a collection of Caesarius's sermons, identified only in 1931, the text of the *Quicunque* appears in full under the title *Fides Sancti Athanasii* (The Faith of St. Athanasius).[21] Caesarius prefaces the Creed with the following description: "We have first of all written out in this collection the Catholic faith itself as the holy fathers defined it, for we ought both ourselves frequently to read it and to instruct others in it."[22] Though scholars have long assumed that Athanasius's name was attached to the Creed at a much later date, J. N. D. Kelly believes there is good reason to conclude that Caesarius himself may have entitled it "the faith of Athanasius." The evidence of the manuscript itself points in this direction, but in addition Caesarius made a habit of compiling work drawn from the fathers and publishing it under their names; in two cases, certain manuscripts indicate that he published his own work under the name of Athanasius.[23] Whether or not Caesarius himself is the actual

18. J. N. D. Kelly, *The Athanasian Creed* (London: A&C Black, 1964), 3: "The view that the creed was the work of Athanasius . . . was universal in the middle ages."
19. Gwynn, *Athanasius of Alexandria*, 183: "In the memory of western Christianity, the prominence of Athanasius owed much to the false attribution of the Athanasian Creed, perhaps almost as much as to the *Life of Antony*."
20. Ibid., 182.
21. The Creed also appears under the longer title *Fides Catholica Sancti Athanasii Episcopi* (The Catholic Faith of St. Athanasius, Bishop). For the groundbreaking discovery of this collection of Caesarius's sermons, see Kelly, *Athanasius Creed*, 35–37.
22. Cited in Robert Wilken, "Introducing the Athanasian Creed," *Currents in Theology and Mission* 6, no. 1 (1979): 5.
23. Kelly, *Athanasian Creed*, 120. Gerald Bray ("Whosoever Will Be Saved: The Athanasian Creed and the Modern Church," in *Evangelicals and Nicene Faith: Reclaiming the Apostolic Witness*, ed. Timothy

author of the Athanasian Creed, he may have been responsible for its title and wide circulation.

The popularity of the *Quicunque* grew apace in the Middle Ages. In the seventh century, it appears in the formal declarations of the fourth Council of Toledo (633) and the Synod of Autun (670); by the eighth century, commentaries on the Creed begin to appear, and the Creed begins to find its way into the liturgy, first within psalters and then as a canticle sung by priests. From the ninth century onward, "we find the Athanasian Creed in regular use throughout Europe in the office."[24] At what point the Athanasian Creed became linked with the Apostles' Creed and the Nicene Creed as the "three creeds" of the church remains unclear, but certainly by the thirteenth century this linkage of the three creeds was firmly in place.[25]

Thomas Aquinas illustrates how the Athanasian Creed was viewed and used in the high scholastic period. Of the approximately thirty references to Athanasius by name in the *Summa Theologiae*, two-thirds refer to the Athanasian Creed, which Thomas receives as coming from Athanasius himself. In one instance, Thomas asks whether it belongs to the Sovereign Pontiff (the pope) to draw up a symbol of faith. The third objection points to Athanasius as a bishop who also drew up a symbol of the faith: "Athanasius was not the Sovereign Pontiff, but patriarch of Alexandria, and yet he published a symbol which is sung in the Church."[26] Responding to this objection, Thomas proposes that

> Athanasius drew up a declaration of faith, not under the form of a symbol, but rather by way of an exposition of doctrine, as appears from his way of speaking. But since it contained briefly the whole truth of faith, it was accepted by the authority of the Sovereign Pontiff, so as to be considered as a rule of faith.[27]

Thomas rightly grasps the expository quality of the *Quicunque*, and though he was mistaken in attributing the Creed to Athanasius, he

George [Grand Rapids: Baker Academic, 2011], 48) offers the following explanation for why Caesarius may have attributed the creed to Athanasius: "Athanasius was a particularly good candidate for this role, because as the acknowledged defender of orthodoxy and foe of Arianism . . . his authority was unchallenged. . . . As Caesarius would have seen it, the text represents what Athanasius would have thought and said had he been alive at the time, and so it made perfect sense to attribute it to him. The attribution was a theological statement, and it must be judged as that, not as historical fact."

24. Kelly, *Athanasian Creed*, 43.
25. Ibid., 44.
26. Thomas Aquinas, *Summa Theologiae*, 2.2.1.10, obj. 3.
27. Ibid., reply 3.

accurately describes its origin and evolution: it was drawn up originally as a concise exposition of the faith and only gradually attained the status of a formal liturgical creed sung in the church.[28]

The medieval tradition of the three creeds was largely accepted by both sides in the Reformation debate. Pope Pius V confirmed the use of the Athanasian Creed in the revised breviary (1568), to be sung at the office of prime on Sundays. The Reformers by and large welcomed the Athanasian Creed as a faithful and useful statement of scriptural truth. In the Lutheran Book of Concord (1580), the *Quicunque* is given equal honor with the Apostles' and Nicene Creeds; the Belgic Confession of the Reformed church (1566) accords it authoritative status; and the Anglican Thirty-Nine Articles declare it as one of the creeds that ought to be received and believed.[29] As we shall see, this reception by the Reformation of a resolutely Trinitarian creed, ostensibly from the pen of Athanasius, would lead to a firm rejection of this Creed when the doctrine of the Trinity came under fire in the seventeenth and eighteenth centuries, and would put the figure of Athanasius directly in the crosshairs.

Doubts about Athanasius's authorship of the Creed surfaced in the sixteenth century but had little immediate impact on its reception. But by the seventeenth century, the arguments against Athanasian authorship proved overwhelming, not least because the Creed's confession that the Spirit proceeds from the Father *and the Son* could not be credibly attributed to Athanasius. "The collapse of the conservative defence was as complete as it was sudden. Henceforth it was taken as settled, in all circles where scholarship prevailed, that Athanasius could not have written the creed."[30] Though use of the *Quicunque* continued especially in the Lutheran and Anglican traditions, from the seventeenth century forward it was no longer received as representing the exact faith of Athanasius.

Given its importance for the reception of Athanasius in the West, some attention to the theology of the Athanasian Creed and its probable sources is warranted. The text of forty-two verses is neatly bound by an introduction and conclusion that act as parallel bookends. They announce the content of the text as "the catholic faith" (*fides catholica*) and caution readers that one's salvation depends on holding to this

28. Kelly, *Athanasian Creed*, 109: "There can be no reasonable doubt about its original character and object. It was drafted as a summary of orthodox teaching for instructional purposes."
29. Ibid., 48–49.
30. Ibid., 4.

faith fully and securely. The main text is divided into two parts that treat the doctrines of the Trinity and the incarnation respectively, with a bridge between them that sums up the Trinitarian section and introduces the incarnational section (vv. 28–29).[31] The opening verses of the Trinitarian section display the basic theology of the Creed:

> This, then, is the Catholic faith: We worship one God in Trinity and Trinity in unity, without confusing the Persons or separating the substance; for indeed the Person of the Father is one, [the Person] of the Son another, [the Person] of the Holy Spirit another; but the divinity of the Father, the Son, and the Holy Spirit is one, their glory equal, and their majesty coeternal.[32]

A striking feature of these lines is the carefully balanced handling of Trinity and unity, of threeness and oneness. The distinctness of the persons receives significant emphasis but is matched by attention to the oneness of the Godhead and the attributes that pertain to it. There is no evidence here of the supposed Western Trinitarian approach that begins with the common essence and then derives the persons.[33] As the exposition unfolds, this neat balance between Trinity and unity continues. As Kelly observes, the Creed refutes two primary heresies, Sabellianism and Arianism, without naming either.[34] The first confused or merged the persons; the second failed to accord full divinity to the Son (and the Spirit). Through careful and balanced phrases, the *Quicunque* upholds the distinction of the persons and the entire divinity of each and, at the same time, the oneness of God. The Trinitarian section ends where it began, by holding in balance Trinity and unity: "Thus in all things, as has been stated above, both Trinity in unity and unity in Trinity must be worshipped." By repeating the terms in reverse order, the Creed refuses to give precedence to either aspect.

A brief section on the incarnation follows (vv. 29–37). Again, the balance of truths marks the text: there is *one* Lord Jesus Christ but he is *both* God and a human being at once. Jesus Christ, the Son of God, is

31. A critical Latin text of the Athanasian Creed with facing English translation is found in Kelly, *Athanasian Creed*, 17–20; Kelly (ibid., 2) lauds the Creed for its intrinsic value: "The creed is one of the most splendid legacies of the patristic age. Whether regarded as literature or as theology, its intrinsic interest is immense."
32. Translation taken from Denzinger, *Compendium of Creeds*, no. 75, adjusted.
33. Recent patristic scholars have strongly rejected the view that the Western theological tradition begins with the one divine essence and derives the persons, while the Eastern theological tradition begins with the persons and works toward the one common essence. For the roots of this faulty paradigm in contemporary theology, see Michel René Barnes, "De Régnon Reconsidered," *Augustinian Studies* 26, no. 2 (1995): 51–79.
34. Kelly, *Athanasian Creed*, 76.

both "perfect man" and "perfect God," equal to the Father in divinity, less than the Father in humanity. Emphasis on the single subject in Christ shines through: "Although he is God and man, [he] is nevertheless not two but one Christ."[35] Kelly persuasively shows that this section is tacitly anti-Nestorian, and so must have been composed after Ephesus and Chalcedon; though the Creed lacks the term *nature* when speaking of Christ's divinity and humanity, it reflects the Christology of the Chalcedonian definition.[36]

Once it was established that the Athanasian Creed was not penned by Athanasius, the hunt was on to detect the real author by means of internal evidence and external attestation.[37] The leading hypotheses have identified three primary candidates: Ambrose of Milan, Vincent of Lérins, and Caesarius of Arles. The parallels with Ambrose are impressive, and at first blush the case for his authorship appears strong. His corpus contains many parallels to the phrases in the *Quicunque*, like the following: "Both the Father is Lord, and the Son is Lord. . . . Yet there are not two Lords, but one Lord. Because both the Father is God and the Son is God; but there is one God."[38] The prime difficulty with this hypothesis is that the parallels with Augustine are even more impressive, as indicated in the following passage from Augustine's *De Trinitate*:

> The Father is God, the Son is God, the Holy Spirit is God; and the Father is good, the Son is good, the Holy Spirit is good; and the Father is omnipotent, the Son is omnipotent, the Holy Spirit is omnipotent: yet there are not three Gods, nor three good, nor three omnipotent, but one who is God, good, omnipotent, the Trinity itself.[39]

For a host of reasons, the search for the author has narrowed the focus to the school of Lérins in Gaul; the Athanasian Creed not only mirrors the writings of the leading lights of this school but the internal evidence involving style, vocabulary, and rhythm confirms the strong likelihood that the Creed was composed in this milieu. Kelly examines in detail the case for both Vincent and Caesarius, concluding that neither was the author but that both probably contributed to the formation of the Creed.[40]

35. Ibid., 20.
36. Ibid., 105.
37. See Kelly, *Athanasian Creed*, 1–14, for the centuries-long effort to ascertain the true author of the Athanasian Creed.
38. Ambrose, *Expositio Evangelii secundum Lucam*, 10.4; cited in Kelly, *Athanasian Creed*, 82.
39. Augustine, *Trin.*, 8.1; cited in Kelly, *Athanasian Creed*, 83. Kelly (*Athanasian Creed*, 80) concludes that the *Quicunque* "can fairly be described as codified and condensed Augustinianism."

Actual authorship aside, the crucial question remains: Does the Athanasian Creed amount to a kind of deceit whereby a theology foreign to Athanasius's thought was smuggled in under his name? Or does the Creed reasonably represent the thought and theology of Athanasius, even if not his precise way of stating it? In other words, did the Western tradition, by receiving this Creed, imbibe a false understanding of Athanasius's "faith," or was his thought fairly represented in the eloquent, balanced cadences that were sung in choir week after week?

If Caesarius of Arles is, in fact, responsible for the title of the Creed, "The Faith of Athanasius," there is no reason to suppose that he was attempting to dupe people by means of a forged authorship. Athanasius was plainly the great hero of Trinitarian faith, the icon who contended for the orthodox understanding of the Triune God. His *Letter to Epictetus* was also recognized in the West as a crucial testimony to the truth of the incarnation. By entitling the *Quicunque* "The Faith of Athanasius," Caesarius may have intended nothing more than to identify "the Catholic faith" concerning the Trinity and the incarnation with the faith of Athanasius, the giant who had contended for both.

But does the Athanasian Creed, in fact, line up with the "faith of Athanasius"? Though the phrasing is different, it is not difficult to see the same faith expressed in the following selection from Athanasius's oration against the Arians: "But they are two, because the Father is Father and is not the Son, and the Son is Son and not the Father, but the nature is one, for the offspring is like its parent, for it is his image. And all that is the Father's is the Son's. Wherefore the Son is not another God."[41] Nearly the same form of expression appears in Athanasius's successor, Cyril of Alexandria:

> The holy and consubstantial Trinity is distinguished by the differences in names and the qualities and attributes of the persons. The Father is the Father and not the Son; the Son is the Son and not the Father; and the Holy Spirit is the Spirit, belonging to the divine nature. Yet the Trinity is summed up in the same essence, giving us not three but one God.[42]

40. Kelly, *Athanasian Creed*, 116–24.
41. Athanasius, *Contra Arianos*, 3.4.1–2; cited in Jon M. Robertson, *Christ as Mediator: A Study of the Theologies of Eusebius of Caesarea, Marcellus of Ancyra, and Athanasius of Alexandria* (Oxford: Oxford University Press, 2007), 220.
42. Cyril of Alexandria, *Commentary on John 14:1*; in *Commentary on John*, vol. 2, trans. David R. Maxwell, ed. Joel C. Elowsky, Ancient Christian Texts (Downers Grove, IL: InterVarsity Press, 2015), 146.

Likewise, the burden of Athanasius's *Letter to Epictetus* is to uphold the real humanity of the Word himself but at the same time to distinguish the divinity of the Word from the human body that he assumed.

> But the Saviour having in very truth become man, the salvation of the whole man was brought about. For if the Word were in the Body putatively, as they say, and by putative is meant imaginary, it follows that both the salvation and the resurrection of man is apparent only. . . . But truly our salvation is not merely apparent, nor does it extend to the body only, but the whole man, body and soul alike, has truly obtained salvation in the Word Himself.[43]

Though the terms are different, Athanasius, like the *Quicunque*, seeks to uphold the single subject in the incarnation (the Word) and, at the same, maintain the full divinity and humanity of the Word.

The inclusion of the phrase "and the Son" (*et filio*) in the Athanasian Creed is more difficult to square with the faith of Athanasius. He did not speculate on the procession of the Spirit and nowhere in his extant works does he assert that the Spirit proceeded from the Father *and the Son*. But nevertheless, in Athanasius (and even more in Cyril) we encounter a conviction that the Spirit is in some way dependent on the Son and that he shines forth "from the Son."

The language of the Athanasian Creed is well downstream from Athanasius: the terminology is for the most part characteristically Western and the author has thoroughly digested the fruits of the christological controversies of the early fifth century. But as Duane Arnold proposes, the Athanasian Creed is in the main faithful to the teaching of Athanasius: "It is perhaps ironic that a work that he did not write helped to preserve Athanasius' legacy [in the West] and indeed to promote many of the theological values that he had fought to defend. The fundamental doctrines of the Quicunque are teachings that Athanasius upheld."[44] If there is one thing missing from the *Quicunque* that characteristically marks "the faith of Athanasius," it is the lack of any mention of salvation and deification. The Athanasian Creed simply sums up the orthodox teaching on the Trinity and incarnation; Athanasius nearly always linked this confession with its goal: the transformation and divinization of the human being.

43. Athanasius, *Ad Epictetum*, 7; in *NPNF*^{2}, 4:572–73.
44. Arnold, *Early Episcopal Career*, 183–84.

Conclusion: Athanasius and the Reformers

A wide translation of Athanasius's works from Greek into Latin occurred in the fifteenth century, fueled by the Renaissance ideal to recover ancient texts.[45] In general, the reception of Athanasius in the early Reformation was shaped by the late medieval Latin tradition; Athanasius was appealed to especially for defense of the doctrine of the Trinity (and in later centuries, in defense against the anti-Trinitarians).[46] Unsurprisingly, given their sharp critique of medieval monasticism, the Reformers paid far less attention to the *Life of Antony* and the call to the ascetic-monastic life. For them, Athanasius was preeminently the great teacher and defender of the doctrine of the Trinity.

For Martin Luther, who engaged in an intensive reading of Athanasius in Erfurt, Athanasius represents above all the authentic witness of faith against heresy; he was the archetype of orthodoxy. Athanasius also serves as an important authority for Philip Melanchthon, who frequently cites *On the Incarnation* as a witness to true Trinitarian and christological thinking.[47] We already noted the acknowledgement of the Athanasian Creed as a true witness to the faith in the Lutheran, Reformed, and Anglican confessions. The one notable exception to this warm reception of Athanasius is John Calvin. He makes no positive use of Athanasius and when pressed about whether he subscribed to the three creeds, replied that he "had pledged his faith to the one God, not to Athanasius whose creed had never been approved by any true church."[48]

For the Reformers, the translation of Athanasius's corpus into Latin was not a landmark event as was the publication of the Greek New Testament. They were not so much captivated by a rediscovery of the fathers for their own sake as they were interested in gathering from the patristic texts testimony to the truths of the faith and the reforms of the church they sought to enact. They largely received the teaching and portrait of Athanasius handed on to them by the medieval tradition, and so viewed him as a beacon of orthodox teaching who taught and contended for the biblical revelation of the Triune God and the

45. See Gemeinhardt, *Athanasius Handbuch*, 440–41. Jaroslav Pelikan (*The Christian Tradition*, vol. 4, *Reformation of Church and Dogma [1300–1700]* [Chicago: University of Chicago Press, 1984], 77) identifies the humanist monk Ambrose Traversari (1386–1439) as a translator of the Greek fathers into Latin.

46. Gemeinhardt, *Athanasius Handbuch*, 443.

47. Ibid., 442–43.

48. John Calvin, *Ep.* 49, in Maurice Wiles, *Archetypal Heresy: Arianism through the Centuries* (New York: Oxford University Press, 1996), 54.

incarnation of the Son of God. Others would follow, however, who would, with close inspection, work through the texts of Athanasius, and who would identify him either as the champion of Christian orthodoxy or the arch-heretic who turned the church in the wrong direction.

6

Contra and Pro Athanasius: Isaac Newton and John Henry Newman

Newton sought to show, not only that Athanasius was the author of "the whole fornication"—that is, of trinitarianism . . .—but also that Athanasius was a depraved man ready even to use murder to promote his ends.[1]

For Newman, Athanasius was "the champion of the truth."[2]

Isaac Newton and John Henry Newman represent two diametrically opposed receptions of the teaching and figure of Athanasius. Newton, the great astronomer, kept his passionately critical views of Athanasius out of the public eye, but his private writings and personal conversations appear to have aided and abetted the English Arian movement of the eighteenth century. More than a century later, Newman, the great scholar and preacher, made no secret of his admiration for Athanasius. For the former, Athanasius represented all that went wrong in the church; he is the villain and arch-heretic in the story of the church's downfall. For the latter, Athanasius was the great champion of the faith and the model for how current struggles were to be carried out.

This narrative, contra and pro Athanasius, concentrates on these

1. Richard S. Westfall, *The Life of Isaac Newton* (Cambridge: Cambridge University Press, 1993), 136–37.
2. Ian Ker, *John Henry Newman: A Biography* (Oxford: Clarendon, 1988), 50.

two prominent figures, but each operated within a wider movement: Newton at the front end of the English Arian current and Newman within the Oxford movement. In both currents, Athanasius functions as a principal iconic figure; in a sense, he is "made present" in a striking way, stirring up passionate responses and functioning as an emblem around which contemporary struggles were fought out. In both currents, the teaching and character of Athanasius stand or fall together. In these contrasting positions, we possess a sketch of what will appear in the twentieth-century battles over the orthodoxy and the reputation of the embattled patriarch of Alexandria.

Isaac Newton and the British Arians

Despite the consistent testimony of biographers in the past two generations, it comes as a great surprise when people learn that Isaac Newton (1642–1727) spent nearly as much time reading and writing about "divinity" or "theology" as he did on mathematics, optics, and astronomy. A vast collection of Newton's unpublished papers came to light only in the twentieth century; they reveal a man consumed with biblical, prophetic, and theological issues.[3] Notably for our purposes, Athanasius figures prominently in Newton's theological odyssey.

Around the age of thirty, while serving as a fellow of Trinity College in Cambridge and holding the Lucasian Chair of Mathematics, Newton became passionately interested in biblical and theological questions. Biographer Richard Westfall identifies this as Newton's "massive commitment" to theology.[4] The requirement for fellows of the college to take orders in the Church of England probably spurred Newton to revisit his religious convictions. With the same independent and scrutinizing method he applied to science and mathematics, Newton began to scour biblical texts and to read works of early Christian writers. "[Newton] followed his established method. He studied the documentary evidence, analysed it, and then produced his own deductions in a notebook divided into headings."[5] Gathering up more than thirty translations of the Bible and learning basic Hebrew, Newton became a student of the Scriptures.[6] "Almost the first fruit of New-

3. For the history of Newton's unpublished papers, see Sarah Dry, *The Newton Papers: The Strange and True Odyssey of Isaac Newton's Manuscripts* (Oxford: Oxford University Press, 2014). Most of Newton's unpublished papers are undated and often several versions of the same work appear. In all, Newton's unpublished papers contain approximately 1.4 million words dedicated to biblical, theological, and historical topics.
4. Westfall, *Life of Isaac Newton*, 120.
5. Michael White, *Isaac Newton: The Last Sorcerer* (Reading, MA: Addison-Wesley, 1997), 152.

ton's theological study was doubt about the status of Christ and the doctrine of the Trinity."[7] Newton quickly became convinced that the traditional Christian teaching on the full divinity of Christ and the Trinitarian understanding of God was deeply flawed, based as it was (in his view) on forged texts and misguided exegesis.

From his study of the Scriptures, Newton turned to the writings of the early church fathers. "Newton set himself the task of mastering the whole corpus of patristic literature. . . . There was no single patristic writer of importance whose works he did not devour. And always his eye was on the allied problems of the nature of Christ and the nature of God."[8] He read both the Latin and Greek fathers, but there is some doubt about Newton's proficiency in Greek; he appears to have relied mainly on Latin translations of the Greek fathers.[9] Still, his determination to examine the original sources shows an admirable determination to investigate theological questions with thoroughness.

From his readings in the church fathers, Newton adopted a clear and radical interpretation that lined up with his previous biblical study: Athanasius was wrong and Arius was fundamentally right. Newton

> became fascinated with the man Athanasius and with the history of the church in the fourth century, when a passionate and bloody conflict raged between Athanasius and his followers, the founders of what became Christian orthodoxy, on the one hand, and Arius and his followers, who denied the trinity and the status of Christ in the Godhead, on the other.[10]

For Newton, the history of the church reached a crisis point in the fourth century. It was here that the more primitive and non-Trinitarian view of God and Christ that Newton discovered in the early second- and third-century fathers ran aground against the novelties of Athanasius and his supporters. "Newton concluded that Athanasius had perpetrated a fraud. He had interpolated key words into the sacred Scriptures to support his argument that Christ was God. In that endeavour he had been supported by the Church of Rome."[11] For Newton,

6. Peter Ackroyd, *Newton* (London: Chatto & Windus, 2006), 52.
7. Westfall, *Life of Isaac Newton*, 121.
8. Ackroyd, *Newton*, 122.
9. Scott Mandelbrote ("Newton and Eighteenth-Century Christianity," in *The Cambridge Companion to Newton*, ed. I. Bernard Cohen and George E. Smith [Cambridge: Cambridge University Press, 2002], 416) concludes that "Newton's Greek was probably not good enough to allow him to cope easily with the original versions." Mandelbrote also points to evidence that Newton relied on collections of quotations from other writers in order to compile his history of the early church.
10. Westfall, *Life of Isaac Newton*, 122.
11. Ackroyd, *Newton*, 53–54.

the axis of error was Athanasius in league with Rome: "Newton held that the pope in Rome had aided and abetted Athanasius and that the idolatrous Roman church was the direct product of Athanasius' corruption of doctrine."[12] In Newton's view, the church that traces its descent from Athanasius and the Nicene Creed had it exactly backward. Rather than Arius being the arch-heretic and Athanasius the champion of Christian truth, Newton concluded that Athanasius was the arch-heretic and Arius the (largely) faithful expositor of an early and purer non-Trinitarian faith.[13] Newton clarifies in his notes that the fundamental error in worshiping Christ as God is the sin of idolatry. It amounts to a charge of blasphemy against the church's Nicene confession of faith. "To Newton a commitment to trinitarianism was tantamount to blasphemy."[14]

Newton did not stop just with a critique of Athanasius's teaching; he sought to expose his flawed character as well in a treatise entitled "Paradoxical Questions Concerning the Morals and Actions of Athanasius and His Followers," which appears in Newton's unpublished papers. For Newton, "It is the character as well as the doctrine of Athanasius that was suspect."[15]

> Newton virtually stood Athanasius in the dock and prosecuted him for a litany of sins. . . . Newton sought to show, not only that Athanasius was the author of "the whole fornication"—that is, of trinitarianism, "the cult of the three equal Gods"—but also that Athanasius was a depraved man ready even to use murder to promote his ends.[16]

All this made Newton deeply uneasy with the prospect of taking orders in an Anglican Church that upheld the very Trinitarianism he rejected. In the judgment of Richard Westfall, "well before 1675, Newton had become an Arian in the original sense of the term. He recognized Christ as a divine mediator between God and humankind, who was subordinate to the Father who created him."[17] Michael White concurs: "Sometime between 1672 and 1675, Newton set out twelve points of faith

12. Westfall, *Life of Isaac Newton*, 124.
13. Frank E. Manuel (*The Religion of Isaac Newton: The Fremantle Lectures of 1973* [Oxford: Clarendon, 1974], 58) believes that Newton was more intent on casting Athanasius as the villain than Arius as the hero: "While Newton's chief villain in the history of the Church was Athanasius rather than Arius, he censured both for having introduced metaphysical subtleties into their disputes and corrupted the plain language of Scripture."
14. White, *Isaac Newton*, 150.
15. Wiles, *Archetypal Heresy*, 101.
16. Westfall, *Life of Isaac Newton*, 136–37.
17. Ibid., 124.

that formed the foundations of his Arianism."[18] Through the agency of friends, Newton sought an exemption from the requirements of orders, and to the evident surprise of himself and others, this exemption was granted in perpetuity for the office holder of the Lucasian Chair in Mathematics. In the end, Newton was able to retain his academic positions without being required to publicize his heterodox Christian views.

Newton was fascinated as well with biblical prophecy, demonstrated by the fact that he composed four separate commentaries on Daniel and Revelation.[19] "He pored over the prophets, tracing the path of their utterance through symbols and hieroglyphs. He believed that in their words could be found hidden truths concerning the future history of the world."[20] Notably, he identified the "beast" in Revelation not only with the Roman Church (a common identification among Protestants in his day), but specifically with the figure of Athanasius and the promulgation of the Nicene Creed in 381. In Newton's view, the false teaching propagated by Athanasius and others that reached its culmination in the Creed of 381 represents the opening of the seventh seal, unleashing the judgments of the seven trumpets to follow. The mystery of blasphemy written on the forehead of the Whore of Babylon is the doctrine of the Trinity, introduced by Athanasius as a new form of polytheism.[21] For Newton, "the Great Apostasy was no longer Romanism; it was trinitarianism,"[22] and this apostasy continued to his own day; even in the reformed churches, the specter of Trinitarianism remained. "The false religion and idolatry introduced during the fourth century had been perpetuated by the Catholic Church and survived even in the reformed Church of England of Newton's day."[23] Newton's reading and application of biblical prophecy not only confirmed his conclusions drawn from biblical and historical studies but also produced the conviction that he was part of a small, faithful remnant that held to the original truth. "There is no doubt that Newton placed himself among the select few."[24]

Isaac Newton's fascination with religious questions was not limited to his young adulthood. He maintained interest in these questions and

18. White, *Isaac Newton*, 149.
19. Manuel, *Religion of Isaac Newton*, 11.
20. Ackroyd, *Newton*, 55.
21. Maurizio Mamiani, "Newton on Prophecy and the Apocalypse," in *The Cambridge Companion to Newton*, ed. I. Bernard Cohen and George E. Smith (Cambridge: Cambridge University Press, 2002), 394.
22. Westfall, *Life of Isaac Newton*, 126.
23. Mandelbrote, "Newton," 420.
24. Westfall, *Life of Isaac Newton*, 128.

returned to them throughout his life. In the latter decades of the seventeenth century, Newton produced sketches of an overall historical narrative of the church. In a treatise called "The Philosophical Origins of Gentile Theology," Newton theorized on the origins of religious belief and the fall from a pure knowledge of God possessed by Noah and his sons. "Much of Newton's unpublished theological scholarship was devoted to elucidating the history of that Church, from its reestablishment by Noah to its most recent corruption by Athanasius and his papal successors."[25] In this narrative, the land of Egypt serves as the place of ultimate corruption. It is there that idolatry, the fundamental sin, grew and developed. Unsurprisingly, Newton links Egypt's original corrupting role in his history of religion with the figure of Athanasius. In Athanasius, pagan idolatry arises once again: "Through Athanasius, Egypt once again played its nefarious role as the corrupter of true religion."[26]

Standing back and surveying Newton's theological writings, we can recognize a striking triangulation that points to Athanasius as the chief antagonist. Whether from Newton's doctrinal reading of Scripture and interpretation of biblical prophecy, his interpretation of the fathers, or his broader theory of religious development, all roads lead to the mischief caused by Athanasius and the tragic triumph of Trinitarianism. Athanasius functions in Newton's fall narrative of the church as the epicenter and icon of all that went wrong. And Newton saw himself as part of the faithful remnant who were preserving the truth in an age of apostasy.

Why, then, did Newton not take a public stand in favor of an Arian view of Christian belief or seek to renew the church and purge it of Trinitarianism? Why is it that "in public Newton chose to disguise his heterodoxy" and "concealed his views so effectively that only in our day has full knowledge of them become available"?[27] The dominant reason proposed is that Newton kept his theological views hidden because if he had revealed them, he would have lost his university appointments and place in society. "If Newton had admitted his faith he would have been stripped of his university appointments. . . . He reserved his theological conversations for fellow believers."[28] This was not an idle fear; several of Newton's friends and colleagues published

25. Mandelbrote, "Newton," 421.

26. Ibid., 140. White (*Isaac Newton*, 153–54) identifies Newton's passionate distaste for Trinitarianism and his abhorrence of the Roman Church as the twin obsessions that run through his notes on the history of the church.

27. Westfall, *Life of Isaac Newton*, 238, 135.

their Arian views and promptly lost their posts. In short, Newton hid his theological views to preserve his place in society.

Two other motives, however, may have played a role in Newton's secrecy. On the one hand, he may have refrained from publishing his views not just to maintain his position in society but also because he thought the days of Trinitarianism were passing; the best strategy was to be patient and let it pass of its own accord.[29] On the other hand, Newton believed that he belonged to a remnant singled out to preserve the truth for the church, but he also concluded that the prophecies in Daniel were yet to be fulfilled and the time had not yet come for the overturning of heresy in the church. For either or both of these reasons, Newton may have judged the time inexpedient for publicizing his theological commitments.

Isaac Newton was not the lone Arian adherent in his day. In his study of Arianism through the ages, Maurice Wiles dedicates the larger part of the volume to "the rise and fall of British Arianism" in the eighteenth century.[30] Notably, for this select group, "the archetypal heresy was Athanasian orthodoxy, and what the fourth-century fathers called 'Arianism' was the true embodiment of 'primitive Christianity.'"[31] After identifying strands of Arianism in the early seventeenth century, Wiles offers his own account of what he calls "the secret Arianism of Isaac Newton."[32] For Wiles, it is conceptually important to distinguish Arian views of Christ from those termed Socinian or Unitarian. All share a rejection of Trinitarianism, but the crucial feature of the Arian view is the conviction that the Son is preexistent and, though a creature, participates to an eminent degree in divinity. In Wiles's view, Newton went further than his distinguished contemporary John Locke by affirming "the pre-existent Christ as a distinct being of a secondary divine nature."[33] Nonetheless, Wiles concludes that "Newton's attitude emerges as passionately anti-Athanasian rather than pro-Arian. Arius is a figure of no great importance to him."[34]

28. Ackroyd, *Newton*, 54. According to Sarah Dry (*Newton Papers*, 20), this is also why Newton's heirs kept his theological writings away from the public eye.
29. Manuel, *Religion of Isaac Newton*, 63.
30. Wiles, *Archetypal Heresy*.
31. Ibid., 5.
32. Ibid., 77–93.
33. Ibid., 83. Scholars differ on the precise impact Newton may have had on the theological convictions of John Locke. Wiles finds "at least an incipient Arian style of belief" in Locke (ibid., 75), but doubts that Newton confided in Locke regarding his Arian—and anti-Athanasian—views (ibid., 76). But Westfall (*Life of Isaac Newton*, 199–203) and Mandelbrote ("Newton," 410) believe Newton shared his explicitly Arian views with Locke.
34. Wiles, *Archetypal Heresy*, 92.

Two leading figures in the British Arian movement, William Whiston and Samuel Clarke, were students and close confidants of Isaac Newton. Both probably gained (or were strengthened in) their commitments to an Arian view of Christ through their contact with Newton.[35] William Whiston (1677–1752) succeeded Newton—at Newton's own recommendation—to the Lucasian Chair in Mathematics in 1703. In contrast to Newton, he publicized his adherence to an Arian form of belief, resulting in his dismissal from his academic posts in 1710. He never again enjoyed gainful employment.

Whiston believed that primitive Christianity, before its corruption, was basically Arian in belief: "I am abundantly satisfied that the Arian doctrines are those delivered by our Saviour and his Apostles and all the first Christians."[36] Whiston traces the turn away from this primitive faith to Tertullian, but the true villain of his fall narrative is the later Athanasius, who blurred the distinction of the Father and Son and failed to uphold that the Father alone is really and truly God. Interestingly, the hero of Whiston's narrative is not Arius himself, but Eunomius, the chief theological expositor of so-called neo-Arianism in the second half of the fourth century. Whiston labelled the Athanasian Creed "the most heretical creed now extant in the world," preferring instead the longer Creed of Eunomius, which for Whiston was "full, plain, distinct, judicious, and agreeable to the original doctrines of Christianity."[37] Following in the steps of Newton, his mentor, Whiston published a list of seventeen *Suspicions Concerning Athanasius*, describing him as an "ignorant and pernicious heretic" and "a notorious forger and liar."[38] Once again, Athanasius serves as the archvillain in the story of the corruption of the Christian faith.

Samuel Clarke provided a scholarly grounding for the British Arian movement through the publication of the *Scripture-Doctrine of the Trinity* (1712). He studiously recommended a moderate form of Arianism, offering conclusions less radical and abrasive than Whiston but tending in the same direction. "What Newton had cogitated in his inner chamber and Whiston had shouted from the house-tops, Clarke was now promulgating in the measured tones of reasoned exposition."[39] He was so bold as to attempt to show that the Athanasian Creed itself, a regular part of the Anglican liturgy, was compatible with

35. Ibid., 93.
36. Cited in Wiles, *Archetypal Heresy*, 95.
37. Ibid., 104.
38. Ibid., 101.
39. Ibid., 112.

his moderate form of Arianism. His efforts mainly had the effect of encouraging other Arian-sympathizers to jettison the Athanasian Creed altogether.[40] Clarke was formally charged with anti-Trinitarian heresy by the lower house of the Anglican clergy in 1714, but due to support by several bishops and his own partial retraction of his views, the case was dismissed.[41]

The story of Isaac Newton and the British Arian movement furnishes a fascinating window onto the reception of Athanasius. The tables are turned, the terms are reversed. Arius and Eunomius are vindicated as authentic representatives of primitive Christian faith. Athanasius functions as the icon of all that went wrong: his teaching and character are equally vilified and repudiated. The great champion of orthodoxy becomes the arch-heretic and epicenter of the church's fall from truth. In Isaac Newton, we encounter a forerunner of the anti-Athanasian sentiment of the twentieth century and an apt foil for the pro-Athanasian reception by John Henry Newman.

John Henry Newman and the Oxford Movement

If, as a general assessment, the Western Christian tradition did not have a wide acquaintance with the actual writings of Athanasius, the same cannot be said of John Henry Newman (1801–90). "There was perhaps no one in any country who, in the first half of the nineteenth century, had a greater knowledge of Athanasius than Newman."[42] Tracing the history of his own religious development, Newman recounts that at the age of fifteen he "drew up a series of texts in support of each verse of the Athanasian Creed."[43] This early attachment to the Athanasian Creed suffered a relapse during Newman's early years as a tutor at Oriel College in Oxford. As Rowan Williams observes, "Newman himself says . . . that he was at first cool towards the language of post-Nicene theology, not enthusiastic for the Athanasian Creed, and disposed to prefer the ante-Nicene authorities."[44] Newman admits that in 1827 he was "drifting in the direction of liberalism" and found the Athanasian Creed "unnecessarily scientific." "I was just then very strong for that ante-Nicene view of the Trinitarian doctrine, which

40. Ibid., 115.
41. Manuel, *Religion of Isaac Newton*, 7.
42. Cross, *Study of St. Athanasius*, 10.
43. John Henry Newman, *Apologia Pro Vita Sua* (Garden City, NY: Doubleday, 1956), 128.
44. Rowan Williams, "Newman's *Arians* and the Question of Method in Doctrinal History," in *Newman after a Hundred Years*, ed. Ian Kerr and Alan G. Hill (Oxford: Clarendon, 1990), 263.

some writers, both Catholic and non-Catholic, have accused of wearing a sort of Arian exterior."[45] This posture would soon change dramatically, in part because in the following year Newman began a thorough, chronological reading of the church fathers, beginning with Ignatius of Antioch and Justin Martyr. Newman describes this as the return to "my early devotion towards the Fathers."[46]

The role that Athanasius and the fathers of the church played in Newman's thought and imagination cannot be grasped apart from the sense of mission that Newman himself so powerfully describes in his *Apologia Pro Vita Sua*. Provoked by what he saw as the interference by the State in the life of the Anglican Church, and animated by the ideas and convictions of associates such as John Keble and Hurrell Froude, Newman believed himself to be caught up in the defense of the church and of the faith in his time. Notably, the Arian controversy of the fourth century—and especially the figure of Athanasius—became the primary lens through which he viewed and interpreted the fight for the truth in his own day.

In 1830, Newman received a commission to write a short work on the Council of Nicaea. This launched him on a study of the entire period, resulting in a volume of 422 pages entitled *The Arians of the Fourth Century* that appeared in 1833. In the introduction, Newman argues that Antioch, not Alexandria, is the originator of Arian doctrine. His nuanced and critical defense of Alexandrian theology and its key figures (Clement, Origen, Dionysius) reveals his attachment to Alexandrian theology.[47] Newman's description of Athanasius in *Arians* reads very much like that in Nazianzen's oration of old. Athanasius is depicted as "the great Egyptian prelate," calmly prosecuting the work for which he was raised up.[48] The character and virtue of Athanasius receive special notice: "While he punished, he spared, and restored in the spirit of meekness, while he rebuked and rejected with power." "It is this union of opposite excellences, firmness with discrimination and discretion, which is the characteristic praise of Athanasius."[49] What so many have found to be incompatible traits in Athanasius—his fierceness and his kindness—Newman combines into one integrated mindset and character: "Deliberate apostasy and systematic heresy were the

45. Newman, *Apologia*, 135.
46. Ibid., 145.
47. As Rowan Williams ("Newman's *Arians*," 280) recognizes, "In 'Arians' Newman thus sets out to vindicate Alexandria in as thoroughgoing way as possible."
48. John Henry Newman, *The Arians of the Fourth Century*, 3rd ed. (London: E. Lumley, 1871), 335.
49. Ibid., 136, 367.

objects of his implacable opposition; but in his behavior towards individuals, and in his judgment of the inconsistent, whether in conduct or creed, he evinces an admirable tenderness and forbearance."[50]

For Newman, however, Athanasius and the early fathers were more than just models to praise and admire. They provided inspiration for what was needed in Newman's time; they served as "icons" for how Newman and others should act in their own struggles against similar opponents and heterodoxies. The final page of *Arians* reveals this typological role, this "making-present" of the heroes of old:

> And so of the present perils, with which our branch of the Church is beset, as they bear a marked resemblance to those of the fourth century, so are the lessons, which we gain from that ancient time, especially cheering and edifying to Christians of the present day. . . . We . . . may rest in the confidence, that, should the hand of Satan press us sore, our Athanasius and Basil will be given us in their destined season, to break the bonds of the Oppressor, and let the captives go free.[51]

In a letter written in the same year, Newman wrote in exasperation: "If only we had one Athanasius, or Basil, we could bear with 20 Eusebiuses."[52] And in verses written in honor of Athanasius (in 1832), Newman calls for a champion like Athanasius to appear in the north:

> When shall our northern Church her champion see,
> Raised by high heaven's decree,
> To shield the ancient faith at his own harm?[53]

Stephen Thomas suggests that in regard to the final sentence in Newman's *Arians*, "it is tempting to conclude that he saw *himself* as such an Athanasius or Basil *redivivus*."[54] Perhaps—but at the very least Newman derived intense inspiration from Athanasius and others, specifically for how they conducted themselves with firmness and charity in a time of great apostasy in the church.

For Newman, the typological role of Athanasius (and the fathers) shifted as his own religious views developed.[55] The first phase occurred in the earliest days of the Oxford movement. The Arians of the fourth

50. Ibid., 367.
51. Ibid., 406.
52. Ker, *John Henry Newman*, 83.
53. Ibid., 56.
54. Stephen Thomas, *Newman and Heresy: The Anglican Years* (Cambridge: Cambridge University Press, 1991), 50.
55. Thomas (*Newman and Heresy*, 255) identifies these as Newman's "three rhetorics of heresy."

century corresponded to the nineteenth-century liberals in the Church of England, "tamperers and accommodators, whose purpose [was] to modify the Christian tradition in the direction of infidelity."[56] Athanasius and the other fathers represented the dogmatic principle in Christianity, faithful to the tradition's reading of Scripture as recognizing the full divinity of the Son. The second phase emerged with the Oxford movement in full swing, as Newman read more thoroughly in the fathers and began to identify Anglicanism as the *via media* between Protestantism and Rome. The true middle way was sketched by the path of orthodoxy that Athanasius and others charted between the twin errors of Sabellianism and Apollinarianism. In a third phase, as Newman's hopes for the *via media* crashed to the ground in the late 1830s, two distinct typologies appeared that yielded the same conclusion. The first emerged through Newman's study of the Monophysites of the fifth century: "I saw my face in that mirror, and I was a Monophysite. The Church of the *Via Media* was in the position of the Oriental communion, Rome was, where she now is; and the Protestants were the Eutychians."[57]

The second typology appeared shortly afterward, while Newman was translating Athanasius for the Library of the Fathers series: "I saw clearly, that in the history of Arianism, the pure Arians were the Protestants, the semi-Arians were the Anglicans, and that Rome now was what it was. The truth lay, not with the *Via Media*, but in what was called "the extreme party."[58]

In his *Essay on the Development of Christian Doctrine*, completed in 1845, the year he left the Anglican Church for Rome, Newman found guidance from Athanasius (among others) for where to locate the true church:

> On the whole, all parties will agree that, of all existing systems, the present communion of Rome is the nearest approximation in fact to the Church of the Fathers, possible though some may think it, to be nearer still to that Church on paper. Did St. Athanasius or St. Ambrose come suddenly to life, it cannot be doubted what communion he would take to be his own.[59]

56. Ibid., 39.
57. Newman, *Apologia*, 217.
58. Ibid., 239.
59. John Henry Newman, *An Essay on the Development of Christian Doctrine*, ed. Charles F. Harrold (New York: Longmans, Green, 1949), 90.

Lecturing five years later to the Catholic University in Ireland, Newman offers an even more comprehensive typology drawn from the figures of the fourth and fifth centuries:

> It is impossible to resist the conclusion, which the actual inspection of the history in detail forces upon us, that what the See of Rome was then such is it now; that what Arius, Nestorius, or Eutyches were then, such are Luther and Calvin now; what the Eusebians or Monophysites then, such the Anglican hierarchy now; what the Byzantine Court then, such is now the Government of England. . . . That ancient history is not dead, it lives; it prophesies of what passes before our eyes; it is founded in the nature of things; we see ourselves in it, as in a glass.[60]

The last sentence is deeply revealing of Newman's manner of applying the controversies in the time of the fathers to the present. Athanasius, Arius, and the others function like prophets to his own day; they are a living mirror in which he can view the figures and controversies of his time.

Rowan Williams points to the dangers of making the controversies of the past the lens through which we interpret the present, and he finds fault with Newman's historical analysis of the Arian conflict and with the way Newman applies fourth-century categories to his own day. But Williams then proceeds to make just such an application of Athanasius to the twentieth century: "Newman's essay on Arianism demonstrates how fatally easy it is to settle on misleading contemporary parallels for the fourth-century crisis; but the risk is still worth taking."[61] Williams then proceeds to draw a correspondence between the fourth century and the German church struggle during the Nazi era in the twentieth century, with Karl Barth playing the figure of Athanasius.[62] For Williams, there is "a certain irresistible parallel between Athanasius and Barth."[63] The temptation to view Athanasius as a paradigmatic, iconic figure and to "apply him" to one's own day seems difficult to resist, even for those who profess dangers and problems with this kind of typological reading of history.

Such is Newman's typological reading of Athanasius and the fourth century. But Newman also drew crucial elements from Athanasius's teaching that became fundamental building blocks of his own theology,

60. John Henry Newman, *Certain Difficulties Felt by Anglicans in Catholic Teaching*, vol. 1 (New York: Longmans, Green, 1908), 379 (lecture 12.5).
61. Rowan Williams, *Arius: Heresy and Tradition*, rev. ed. (Grand Rapids: Eerdmans, 2001), 237.
62. Ibid., 237–38.
63. Ibid., 238.

three of which I will draw attention to here. The first is what Newman identifies as Athanasius's method of reading Scripture within an authoritative tradition. Toward the end of his life, while working on a new translation of Athanasius's anti-Arian orations, Newman offers extended commentary on the Alexandrian and, in the following selection, draws attention to the interplay of Scripture and tradition:

> The fundamental idea with which [Athanasius] starts in the controversy is a deep sense of the authority of Tradition, which he considers to have a definitive jurisdiction even in the interpretation of Scripture, though at the same time he seems to consider that Scripture, thus interpreted, is a document of final appeal in inquiry and in disputation.[64]

The principle of antiquity always weighed heavily with Newman; it was the primary principle on which he originally fixed his hope for justifying the catholicity of the Anglican communion. But in the end, antiquity alone did not suffice; Newman recognized the need for an authoritative tradition and seems to have learned from Athanasius how such a tradition functions in controversy, enabling Scripture to stand as the final appeal while at the same time providing the context for grasping the true sense of the Scripture.

Second, Newman gained foundational insight and inspiration from Athanasius—and from the Athanasian Creed—for his understanding of the doctrines of the Trinity and the incarnation. In Newman's eyes, Athanasius's teaching on the Trinity remains the standard for the church. "This renowned Father is in ecclesiastical history the special doctor of the sacred truth which Arius denied, bringing it out into shape and system so fully and luminously that he may be said to have exhausted his subject, as far as it lies open to the human intellect."[65] Elsewhere, Newman distinguishes between expositing the doctrine of the Trinity and working out its aspects in technical language. He believes Athanasius's achievement was primarily in exposition of the doctrine of the Trinity: "Thus St. Athanasius himself is more powerful in statement and exposition than in proof."[66] In a similar way, Newman drew on both Athanasius and Cyril for undergirding the teaching of Chalcedon and upholding the full divinity of Christ. "[Newman] emphasized Christ's divinity because he judged that to be at risk. For

64. John Henry Newman, *Select Treatises of Athanasius in Controversy with the Arians*, vol. 2 (London: Longmans, Green, 1903), 51.
65. Ibid.
66. Newman, *Essay on the Development*, 178.

that reason, he turned to Athanasius and Cyril and the Alexandrian school, whom he found so congenial, to expound a Christology in which the divinity of Christ could never be in doubt."[67]

The bedrock of Newman's thought is what he terms the "dogmatic principle" and he sees the struggle for this principle as one of the main continuities of his thought:

> I have changed in many things: in this I have not. From the age of fifteen, dogma has been the fundamental principle of my religion: I know no other religion; I cannot enter into the idea of any other sort of religion; religion, as a mere sentiment, is to me a dream and a mockery.[68]

It cannot be said that Athanasius taught this dogmatic principle to Newman; Newman brought this conviction *to* his reading of Athanasius and probably found Athanasius specially attractive because of his commitment to the dogmas of the faith. Yet, Athanasius's untiring defense of dogmatic truth against such formidable opponents strengthened Newman's own resolve and taught him the fundamental features of the Trinitarian doctrine. Nowhere does Newman ascribe the Athanasian Creed to Athanasius, but he strongly supports the teaching of the Creed and views it as entirely consistent with the faith that Athanasius defended. In a sermon preached on Trinity Sunday during his Anglican period, Newman holds forth on the excellences of the Athanasian Creed as a precise summary of Trinitarian faith and a profound hymn of praise:

> It is in the same spirit that the most precise and systematic of all the Creeds, the Athanasian, is rather, as the form of it shows, a hymn of praise to the Eternal Trinity; it being meet and right at festive seasons to bring forth before our God every jewel of the Mysteries entrusted to us, to show that those of which He gave us we have lost none.[69]

A third element that Newman drew from Athanasius is the doctrine of deification. Many commentators have noted Newman's great attraction to the Greek fathers and his assimilation of aspects of Greek patristic theology.[70] Newman himself praises Athanasius for this teaching on

67. Roderick Strange, "Newman and the Mystery of Christ," in *Newman After a Hundred Years*, ed. Ian Kerr and Alan G. Hill (Oxford: Clarendon, 1990), 327.
68. Newman, *Apologia*, 163.
69. John Henry Newman, "Sermon 22.2," in *Parochial and Plain Sermons* (San Francisco: Ignatius Press, 1987), 396.
70. For example, Stephen Thomas (*Newman and Heresy*, 130) offers this summary of Newman's theol-

deification and makes his own the notion that the goal of salvation is the deification of the human race:

> The sanctification, or rather the deification of the nature of man, is one main subject of St. Athanasius's theology. Christ, in rising, raises His Saints with Him to the right hand of power. They become instinct with His life, of one body with His flesh, divine sons, immortal kings, gods. He is in them, because He is in human nature; and He communicates to them that nature, deified by becoming His, that them It may deify. He is in them by the Presence of His Spirit, and in them He is seen. . . . For the Word did not suffer loss in receiving a body, that He should seek to receive a grace, but rather He deified that which He put on, nay, gave it graciously to the race of man.[71]

Though Newman does not employ the terminology of deification frequently, his treatises and sermons are suffused with the idea of the indwelling of God through Christ and the Spirit in the lives of Christians. It is a peculiar mark of his writing and preaching.[72]

John Henry Newman identified broadly with the church of the fathers, finding inspiration, wisdom, and solace in many figures. Still, Athanasius may be said to have held pride of place among them. Ian Ker names Athanasius as Newman's "favorite early Father."[73] George Dragas believes that "Athanasius' habits are assimilated by Newman more decisively than the habits of any other Father."[74] It is probably no coincidence that Newman began and ended his career with efforts to translate Athanasius's works. According to Ker, "[Newman] intended the new translation of Athanasius to complete the uniform edition and to be his last published work. The study of St. Athanasius had been his first and was now his last 'passion.'"[75] It is ironic that Newman was unhappy with both his former and latter efforts to bring Athana-

ogy: "Imbued with the Eastern Fathers, his eyes fixed upon a vision of the glorification and deification of humanity, he stresses that the Word constitutes the unity of Christ's person."

71. Newman, *Essay on the Development*, 130–31.

72. See, e.g., John Henry Newman, "Lecture 9," in *Lectures on Justification*, 6th ed. (London: Longmans, Green, 1892), 218–19; and Newman, "Sermon 19.1," in *Parochial and Plain Sermons*, 366. In his study of deification in the Oxford movement, Andrew Louth ("Manhood into God: The Oxford Movement, the Fathers and the Deification of Man," in *Essays Catholic and Radical*, ed. Kenneth Leech and Rowan Williams [London: Bowerdean, 1983], 70–80) connects a reinvigorated doctrine of the Trinity with a doctrine of deification. He traces this link not only in Newman but also in two other leading figures of the movement, John Keble and Edward Pusey, both close collaborators with Newman, and concludes: "So it is no surprise to find that the recovery of the doctrine of deification in the Oxford movement goes hand-in-hand with a recovery of the doctrine of the Trinity" (Louth, "Manhood into God," 76).

73. Ker, *John Henry Newman*, 434.

74. Dragas, *St. Athanasius of Alexandria*, 179.

75. Ker, *John Henry Newman*, 714.

sius into translation. His first attempt in the early 1840s was adversely affected by his own painful wrestling with his place in the Anglican Church; his last effort was interrupted by the invitation to Rome to receive the cardinal's red hat, which, in his words, "spoilt the revision."[76] In the end, Newman was disappointed with his effort to bring Athanasius into fresh translation.

As a young man, Newman entered the fray of theological controversy, by all indications looking to Athanasius as his model and guide. As a much older man, when invited to attend the first Vatican Council, he pleaded his old age, identifying himself with that set of church fathers who did not participate in ecclesiastical councils: "I am too old to learn the ways of other great Saints, as St. Athanasius, St. Augustine, and St. Ambrose, whom I admire, but cannot run with. They are race-horses—I am a broken-kneed poney."[77] Whether stepping forward to emulate Athanasius or standing back in admiration, Newman never lost his high regard for the patriarch who stood in the breach for the faith of the church: "There has been a time in the history of Christianity, when it had been Athanasius against the world, and the world against Athanasius. The need and straitness of the Church had been great, and one man was raised up for her deliverance."[78]

Isaac Newton and John Henry Newman present us with strikingly opposite receptions of the figure of Athanasius. For Newton, Athanasius represented the fundamental disfiguration of Christian doctrine: a deeply unethical man who caused great harm to the church. Newton saw himself standing among those few who recognized this truth and who were waiting for the redemption of the church. For Newman, Athanasius represented a man who stood for the truth against all odds: a profoundly pious man, to be praised for his virtuous conduct. Newman saw himself standing in Athanasius's wake, serving the same ends in his own time, waiting for the emergence of a "northern" Athanasius to turn the tide. These conflicting readings of Athanasius, though often adopted with less personal investment, characterize the reception of Athanasius from Newman's day to our own.

76. Ibid., 725.
77. Ibid., 617.
78. Newman, *Essay on the Development*, 285.

7

Contemporary Readings of Athanasius

> Even today in current international debates it is difficult for historians to avoid projecting their own preconceptions in regard to Christianity, especially in the case of such a striking character in Church history as Athanasius.[1]

The Uncontested Positive Reception of Athanasius by the Churches

An account of the contemporary reception of Athanasius should begin by identifying where Athanasius's contested legacy lies and where it does not. The formal or official reception of Athanasius in the churches—creeds, confessions, feasts, public documents—is unanimously positive. During his own lifetime, controversy surrounded Athanasius: bishops and emperors hotly disputed whether he ought to be received and welcomed as a bishop and a teacher of the faith. But since the Nicene settlement in the late fourth century, there has been little to no controversy within or between the Eastern and Western churches concerning either the orthodoxy or the holiness of Athanasius.

For the Coptic Church especially, but for all the Oriental Orthodox

1. Charles Kannengiesser, "The Athanasian Decade 1974–84: A Bibliographical Report," *Theological Studies* 46, no. 3 (1985): 531.

and Eastern churches, Athanasius remains a beloved father of the church and a primary authority.[2] Among the Byzantine Orthodox, Athanasius is prized as one of the great fathers, even though his theology does not play as significant or central a role as does, for example, that of the Cappadocian fathers and Maximus.[3] The Catholic Church receives Athanasius as a doctor of the church and one of the four great Eastern fathers; he is cited as an authority in the documents of Vatican II and in the latest edition of the Catholic Catechism.[4] Athanasius's feast day is celebrated in the Coptic Church on May 15, in the Eastern Orthodox Churches on January 18, and in the Catholic Church on May 2. It is more difficult to measure the place of Athanasius in the various Protestant communions, but we noted above how Athanasius was warmly received by several of the early Reformers, and the Creed that bore his name was included in several early Protestant confessions.

The legacy of Athanasius reemerged as a point of controversy largely in Western scholarly writing: among church historians, patristic scholars, and theologians. It was in these contexts that the traditional "orthodox" narrative of Athanasius, as received by the churches, was queried and challenged—and the challenge was aimed at both his teaching and his character. The aim of this final chapter is to trace the lines of this challenge to Athanasius's legacy, first in terms of the quality and adequacy of Athanasius's teaching and then in terms of his character and reputation.

The Teaching of Athanasius

Challenges to the excellence or adequacy of Athanasius's teaching can be grouped into three primary subjects: (1) his doctrine of the Triune God, (2) his Christology, and (3) his teaching on salvation, especially his emphasis on deification. Athanasius is best known for defending and defining the full divinity of the Son and the nature of the Christian God as triune. Is his account of God—the Father, Son, and Spirit—as solid and secure as tradition has claimed? Athanasius's *Letter to Epictetus* was granted canonical status at the Council of Chalcedon (in 451) as representing the true teaching of the church on the person of Christ. But does his Christology actually hold together and stand up under

2. Gemeinhardt, *Athanasius Handbuch*, 390–415; Gwynn, *Athanasius of Alexandria*, 184–92.
3. Gemeinhardt, *Athanasius Handbuch*, 416–20.
4. For the citation of Athanasius in the Vatican II documents, see *Lumen Gentium*, 42; *Ad Gentes*, 2; and *Presbyterorum Ordinis*, 4 (all three available on the Vatican website: http://tinyurl.com/39mnh). For Athanasius in the Catechism, see paragraphs 460, 1169, and 1988 of the Catholic Catechism.

scrutiny? Athanasius is also renowned for his doctrine of salvation, describing the purpose of God to rescue the human race through Christ and to bring us to full sanctification and deification. But does his soteriology adequately interpret the New Testament or does it represent a foreign, pagan importation into Christian truth? There is a certain artificiality in treating these topics separately, since the doctrine of the Triune God, of Christ, and of salvation all belong together in one integrated whole, but for the purpose of presenting the contemporary reception of Athanasius it will be helpful to distinguish them and consider them each in turn.

Trinity

For Isaac Newton and the British Arians—and for those who identify with a Unitarian view of God—Athanasius's forceful presentation of the Trinity is simply wrongheaded and false at its root. Their critique, however, is usually not with some specific aspect or element of his Trinitarian teaching; they simply reject this way of reading the New Testament and consider the orthodox way of defining God as both one and three to be misguided. We are concerned here with something different: with contemporary scholars who criticize Athanasius for presenting an inadequate account of the *orthodox* view of the Trinity. This is to ask: in what ways is Athanasius taken to task for failing to express a satisfactory theology of the Christian doctrine of God?

The principal critique is that Athanasius leans toward—or fully adopts—a form of Trinitarian modalism. This is known under the name of Sabellianism and was condemned in the person of Athanasius's friend and colleague Marcellus of Ancyra. A modalist view of the Trinity allows for the *manifestations* of the Father, Son, and Spirit, but either positively denies that there are any real, distinct persons in God or fails to uphold these distinctions and blurs them together in an unvariegated monism. Adolph von Harnack, writing in the late nineteenth century, concludes that Athanasius's view of God was full of contradictions that the Arians were correct to point out; for Harnack, Athanasius was Sabellian at the core.[5] Richard Hanson judges that Athanasius *leans* toward Sabellian modalism but that he was far from holding it in the end. For Hanson, Athanasius lacked a distinct terminology to identify the persons, resulting in a Trinitarian exposition that failed to accentuate personal distinctions in God.[6] More recently, Christopher Beeley

5. Adolf von Harnack, *History of Dogma*, vol. 4, trans. Neil Buchanan (New York: Dover, 1961), 47.

has renewed the charge that Athanasius's Trinitarian theology leans toward modalism: "We can see that Athanasius's Trinitarian doctrine is vulnerable to modalism and that it notably omits the language of hypostasis still current in other Origenist traditions."[7] He admits that at points Athanasius gives attention to the subsistence of the three persons but concludes that "structurally speaking, Athanasius ends up diverting the Origenist heritage in a modalist direction."[8]

It is true that Athanasius's Trinitarian theology lacks a technical term (such as "hypostasis" or "person") to designate what is "three" in God, and to this extent his description of the Trinity does not possess the terminological clarity that comes with the Cappadocians and later writers. But as Thomas Weinandy observes, though Athanasius lacks a clear technical terminology to identify the divine persons, he "does indicate that their own distinct biblical designations establish and confirm that they are each unique with their own unambiguous, discrete and non-interchangeable subjective identities."[9] Furthermore, as Weinandy shows, Athanasius maintains on several occasions that the Father and Son are distinct and can never be confused. For Athanasius, the term *homoousion* guarantees at one and the same time both the unity of the divine nature and the distinctness of the persons. Only if the Son is distinct from the Father does it make logical sense to say that the two are *homoousion*: "Neither do we hold a Son-Father, as do the Sabellians, calling him *monoousion* but not *homoousion*, and thus destroying the existence of the Son. . . . For neither is the Father the Son, nor the Son the Father. For the Father is the Father of the Son, and the Son, Son of the Father."[10] The sheer lengths that Athanasius goes to in order to show the unity yet distinctiveness of the Father and Son—and later of the Spirit—speaks against a Sabellian-leaning view of the Trinity. Nowhere does he indicate, as Marcellus did, that the distinct subsistence of the persons was only for the sake of the saving economy or would come to an end at some point. For Athanasius as for

6. Hanson, *Search for the Christian Doctrine*, 444. Hanson believes that Athanasius, despite his inadequacies, made an important contribution to the Christian doctrine of God: "But when all is said and done it must be conceded that Athanasius' achievement in his doctrinal works was a great one. He established the ongoing search for an adequate Christian doctrine of God on a quite new basis, pulling it away from its traditional preoccupation with the identification of the Son with a principle of Greek philosophy" (ibid., 458).
7. Beeley, *Unity of Christ*, 138.
8. Ibid., 159–60, 168.
9. Weinandy, *Athanasius*, 76–77.
10. Athanasius, *Expositio Fidei*, 2, cited in Weinandy, *Athanasius*, 77.

Origen before him, the Father, Son, and Spirit remain forever distinct even as they together comprise the one God.

Christology

It is within the sphere of Christology that Athanasius receives the sharpest censure from contemporary scholars. Though criticism of Athanasius's doctrine of Christ goes back to the nineteenth century, an appropriate place to anchor the critique of Athanasian Christology is in the widely influential study of patristic Christology by Aloys Grillmeier in 1965.[11] Grillmeier adopts a model of two contrasting paradigms for evaluating christological thought: *Logos-Sarx* and *Logos-Anthropos*. The former conceives of the incarnation as the union of the eternal Word with human flesh, such that the Word functionally takes over the human operations of Christ. The central plank of the *Logos-Sarx* model is the lack of a theological role for the soul of Christ. In contrast, the *Logos-Anthropos* model conceives of the incarnation as the joining of the eternal Word to a full humanity, such that all human capacities are activated, especially the soul of Christ. For Grillmeier, though each model has its strengths and weaknesses, the *Logos-Sarx* model is plainly inferior because it fails to give a theological role to the full humanity of Christ.

When evaluating Athanasius's corpus, Grillmeier concludes that Christ's soul was a physical reality for Athanasius but not a "theological factor" in his christological schema.[12] "We have Athanasius's remarkable procedure of making the 'flesh' of Christ the physical subject of experiences which normally have their place in the soul."[13] Assessing Athanasius's *Tome to the Antiochenes*, a work that specifically identifies a human soul in Christ, Grillmeier grants that the soul of Christ is present, but in a "physical" not "theological" sense.[14] In the end, however, he concedes that for Athanasius, the incarnation meant that "the Logos is man" and rates the Athanasian approach as preferable to that of Antioch because it provides for a unified subject in Christ (the Logos).[15]

11. Grillmeier, *Christ in Christian Tradition*, 193–219. See also ch. 3, n. 14 in this volume.
12. Grillmeier, *Christ in Christian Tradition*, 196.
13. Ibid., 203.
14. Ibid., 215.
15. Ibid., 218–19. Frances Young (*From Nicaea to Chalcedon*, 63–67) concurs with Grillmeier that Athanasius presents a Word-flesh Christology that is functionally Apollinarian and estimates that in all probability Athanasius did not conceive of Christ as possessing a human soul. Nonetheless, she judges that Athanasius considers Christ to be truly human and that, ironically, his quasi-Apollinarian Christology allows for the Word to experience a genuinely human life.

Richard Hanson, in his monumental history of the fourth-century conflict, delivered another shot across the bow of Athanasian Christology. Hanson famously describes Athanasius's approach to the Word and the flesh as amounting to a "space-suit Christology"—that is, for Athanasius the Word's relation to his own body is no closer than an astronaut to his space suit. He agrees with earlier critiques that Athanasius all but ignores the human mind and soul of Christ, and additionally finds no place in Athanasius's portrayal of Christ either for suffering or for the cross. For Hanson, "whatever else the *Logos* incarnate is in Athanasius' account of him, he is not a human being."[16]

The most detailed censure of Athanasian Christology comes from Christopher Beeley, for whom "decentering Athanasius in the grand picture of fourth-century orthodoxy" is an explicit goal.[17] For Beeley, it is not only that Athanasius has no use for the human soul in Christ; the greater fault is that Athanasius's Christ has no real contact with suffering and so with our humanity. By making the body or the flesh of Christ the agent of suffering, emotion, or ignorance in Christ, Athanasius effectively shuts off Christ's humanity—and so ours—from effective contact with the divine nature.[18] His Christ is like a superhero immune from the real impact of death.[19] Beeley acknowledges instances where Athanasius appears to teach a "unitive Christology" but believes these are really indicative of his tacit-Apollinarianism, not a genuinely orthodox Christian account of the unity of Christ.[20] Turning the tables on the scholarly assumption that Athanasius teaches a unitive Christology, Beeley sharply critiques Athanasius's picture of Christ as dualistic and so insufficient for accomplishing human redemption:

> Athanasius's Christology is not, in the end, more unitive than that of others, as it is sometimes imagined to be, for his anti-Arian polemic and his Logos Christology both require that the Word be kept separate from human experience, and that humanity as such be eliminated in order to make room for the Word's dominion. Athanasius imagines divine and human existence as mutually exclusive realms that cannot be brought together without compromising the one or destroying the other.[21]

16. Hanson, *Search for the Christian Doctrine*, 451.
17. Beeley, *Unity of Christ*, 311.
18. Ibid., 134, 153, 155.
19. Ibid., 137.
20. Ibid., 136, 152, 165.
21. Ibid., 165–66.

It is difficult *not* to conclude that Beeley interprets Athanasius's texts in the most unfavorable and unsympathetic way possible. Even when treating the *Letter to Epictetus*, Beeley charges Athanasius with maintaining his "Word-flesh Christology,"[22] failing to mention the numerous times in the letter itself where Athanasius insists that by "flesh" he means "man" (*anthropos*) and that in Christ's case this certainly includes a soul. The *Letter to Epictetus* is sharply anti-Apollinarian and teaches a soteriological Christology in which the entirety of human nature is genuinely assumed by the eternal Word in order to bring about its transformation.

Another line of scholarship, while admitting limitations or shortcomings in Athanasius's view of Christ, defends him against the charge of being a tacit-Apollinarian. In his penetrating study of Athanasius's theology, Khaled Anatolios argues that Athanasius's view of Christ is framed as it is precisely in order to ensure that it is the divine Word who genuinely experiences human life and suffering.[23] For Athanasius, the crucial point of the incarnation is the direct and unmediated relation between the divine Son (and the divine power) and the human race. Through a careful exegesis of Athanasius's texts, Anatolios deflects the charge that Athanasius teaches a "space-suit Christology" and shows how Athanasius, by claiming that the flesh/body of the Word is "proper" to the Word, forges the strongest possible relation between the Word and his assumed humanity:

> Thus the hermeneutical key to understanding Athanasius's Christology is the paradoxical relation between God and the world whereby the total otherness between the two natures is "bridged over" by the initiative of divine grace. Through the incarnation of the Word, and the appropriation of our condition by the divine subject, this "bridge" amounts to our deification through participation in the Logos.[24]

Anatolios sums up the christological achievement of Athanasius: "As Athanasius saw very clearly . . . in Jesus Christ, we are truly and definitively 'joined' to God in a deifying communion."[25] Where Beeley sees in Athanasius's Christology an unbridgeable duality, Anatolios discovers a genuinely bridged, deifying communion.

In a similar way, John Behr rejects the *Logos-Sarx* paradigm for

22. Ibid., 164.
23. Anatolios, *Coherence of His Thought*, 142. See also Weinandy, *Athanasius*, 92–93.
24. Ibid., 83–84.
25. Ibid., 209.

Athanasius's Christology. Admitting a potential imbalance in the way that Athanasius describes Christ as fully God and fully human,[26] Behr nonetheless interprets Athanasius's account of Christ's divine-human constitution, in direct contrast to Beeley, as enabling the Word to genuinely experience suffering in the human body he has assumed:

> The whole being of Jesus Christ is understood, without minimizing its physical reality, in terms of the Word of God, for it is the Word that has become flesh. Finally, as Athanasius makes explicitly clear in the very next sentence, the Word takes a body, not to provide a means of dwelling impassibly in the world, but so that the Word can undergo death in a body capable of dying.[27]

Where Beeley sees Athanasius creating a chasm between the Word and genuine human experience and suffering, Behr believes that Athanasius provides a means by which the Word authentically experiences human suffering: "It is emphatically *not* that one 'part' of him (his body) suffered, while another 'part' (his divinity) remained above suffering; such a resolution would dissolve the paradox. . . . Both of the elements must be maintained and, at the same time, attributed to one and the same subject."[28]

Alvyn Pettersen offers an explanation for why Athanasius emphasizes the divine, rather than the human, in Christ: "Athanasius is not primarily concerned with the anthropology of the Incarnation; his interest is the 'why' rather than the 'what' of Christ's humanity. . . . There is then an absence of stress on the humanity; but it is not underplayed."[29] Rather than viewing this as a dualistic Christology that fails to connect the Word with our humanity, Pettersen interprets Athanasius as presenting a Christology aimed at deification:

> A potentially static view gives way to a dynamic view. Ignorance, fear, suffering and death are admitted, but only to be alleviated. In his dispelling ignorance, lightening suffering and conquering death, there is the divinizing of everyone in Christ. What superficially may appear to be inchoate Docetism is in fact pervasive soteriology.[30]

26. Behr, *Nicene Faith*, part 1, 216, 213.
27. Ibid., 216.
28. Ibid., 221. Peter J. Leithart (*Athanasius* [Grand Rapids: Baker Academic, 2011], 130) grants that there is some evidence in Athanasius for what Hanson calls a "space-suit Christology," but in the end he thinks this does not represent what Athanasius means or believes: "Despite some 'God in a space suit' twists and turns, Athanasius's fundamental Christology is very different, providing thoroughly theological explanations for the limits and passions of Jesus in the Gospel story."
29. Pettersen, *Athanasius*, 109.
30. Ibid., 126.

Soteriology

In their landmark study, *Early Arianism: A View of Salvation* (1981), Robert C. Gregg and Dennis E. Groh launched a formidable challenge to the traditional orthodox reading of the fourth-century struggle between Arius and Athanasius and proposed a new paradigm for viewing this conflict. Rather than placing the emphasis on metaphysics and the ontology of God, they argue that the debates of the fourth century are, at root, a disagreement over the doctrine of salvation. The core issue is "a clash of two soteriologies, each with its own understanding of the spiritual progress or sanctification of believers."[31] The chief distinction is one of will versus nature: in the first version progress is made through willed obedience; in the second, through attachment to an immutable God-man who secures our stability. "It is this Athanasian confidence in the stability of divine nature over and against his fears for the instability of human nature which constitutes the very heart of both his Christology and his soteriology."[32] For Gregg and Groh, the pivotal issue is whether the Son of God is changeable, and in their view Athanasius taught a doctrine of salvation that was captive, at least in part, to a Platonic conception of immutability: "To biblical Platonists like Bishops Alexander and Athanasius such a changeability in the redeemer was unthinkable."[33] The thesis that Arius was foundationally committed to a particular soteriology has not received universal acceptance, but Gregg and Groh succeeded in bringing soteriological issues to the forefront of the study of Arius and Athanasius.

Related to Gregg and Groh's characterization of Athanasian soteriology is a long-standing critique that Athanasius teaches a "physicalist" doctrine of salvation, whereby Christ assumed and healed our nature in himself (through the incarnation), such that the human race is somehow automatically restored by solidarity with this new humanity in Christ. Christopher Beeley expresses what many have found to be defective in Athanasius's view of salvation:

> Athanasius thus presents us with a fairly unique example of what many modern readers have assumed most of the Greek fathers held, namely, divinization and salvation (of a sort) at the point of incarnation rather

31. Robert C. Gregg and Dennis E. Groh, *Early Arianism: A View of Salvation* (Philadelphia: Fortress Press, 1981), 134.
32. Ibid., 176.
33. Ibid., 161.

> than in the passion and resurrection. Likewise, Athanasius presents Christ's saving effects as being universal for humanity as a whole.[34]

The problems with the approach here attributed to Athanasius are twofold. First, this view of salvation seems to depend on a theory that Christ assumed not an individual and concrete human nature but a universal human nature that then has universal (and automatic) effects on all of humanity. But does this not cut the ground out from under the doctrine of the incarnation and the Son's sharing in our actual, concrete humanity? The second perceived problem is that the passion and cross of Christ become secondary and even redundant. If Christ healed and renewed our humanity through the incarnation, what role does the cross actually play in human redemption? According to Richard Hanson, "one of the curious results of this theology of the incarnation is that it almost does away with a doctrine of the Atonement." Athanasius believes in the atonement but cannot really explain why it is needed: "Once the Logos has taken human flesh on himself, in a sense, certainly in principle, redemption is accomplished."[35]

This critique of Athanasian soteriology has been contested. Norman Russell suggests that in Athanasius "a fruitful approach is perhaps to see Christ's humanity as having a *representative* significance. . . . The deification of humanity in principle, however, still leaves salvation to be appropriated by individuals."[36] Russell identifies two parallel lines for deification in Athanasius: the ontological and the ethical. The first is brought about by the incarnation and is made effective through baptism; the second involves growth in virtue and is portrayed most fully in Athanasius's *Life of Antony*.[37] Importantly, Russell points to the sacramental appropriation of salvation in Athanasius's thought: "What is often described as 'physical redemption' is actually transmitted sacramentally."[38] Alvyn Pettersen draws a similar conclusion, that the universal saving significance of Christ's humanity is balanced by a concern for personal appropriation: "Athanasius' Christ is a representative and not a collective figure. This recognition allows Athanasius to do justice

34. Beeley, *Unity in Christ*, 137.
35. Hanson, *Search for the Christian Doctrine*, 450. Beeley (*Unity in Christ*, 135) agrees with this assessment: "Athanasius's apology for the cross is therefore not so much a defense of the crucifixion as it is an explanation of the divine manifestation of the Word and a vindication of divine power *despite* Christ's death, rather than through it."
36. Russell, *Doctrine of Deification*, 171, 173. Russell (ibid., 171n11) helpfully traces this "physicalist" critique of Athanasius in Adolph von Harnack, Jules Gross, and J. N. D. Kelly.
37. Ibid., 184–85.
38. Ibid., 185.

to both the close bond between Christ and all people and his standing over against everyone, working the salvation of all, calling for repentance and ultimately judging everyone."[39] Thomas Weinandy makes the further claim that "Athanasius recognizes that the Son did not take upon himself some untainted generic humanity, but rather he assumed the fallen humanity of the race of Adam."[40]

John Behr offers a reading of Athanasius's classic text *On the Incarnation* that directly counters the claim that Athanasius minimizes the cross and the atonement. In Behr's view, *On the Incarnation* is not so much about the Word taking flesh but is, in fact, an "apology for the Cross."[41] For Athanasius, the term *incarnation* "does not simply refer to the birth of Jesus from Mary . . . but rather refers to this birth when seen from, and then described in, the perspective of the Cross."[42] Behr takes Hanson and other scholars to task for failing to discern Athanasius's meaning, and so for faulting Athanasius for views he does not hold (that is, that redemption is secured simply by virtue of the incarnation). In Behr's view, rather than minimizing the passion and cross of Christ, Athanasius places them at the center of his narrative of salvation: "There is no question but that Athanasius understands the incarnation in terms of the Passion: the Savior takes a body to die, for it is only through death itself that death is overthrown and life resurrected."[43]

In his account of soteriology and the life of grace in Athanasius, Khaled Anatolios rejects the characterizations proposed by Gregg and Groh and instead argues for an integration of divine initiative and human response in Athanasius.[44] The holiness and stability that the Word brings to his own assumed humanity accomplishes this very thing in the lives of Christians. But this is not an automatic effect occurring apart from human effort and striving. Rather, it is precisely because Christians have received the divine life of Christ through the Spirit that they are encouraged and required to strive for holiness. For

39. Pettersen, *Athanasius*, 132.
40. Weinandy, *Athanasius*, 97.
41. Behr, *Nicene Faith*, part 1, 171. Anatolios (*Coherence of His Thought*, 67) arrives at the same conclusion: "[The two-volume work] is conceived and designed with a view to defending the Christian faith that the one who was crucified on the cross is really God."
42. Ibid., 185.
43. Ibid., 197.
44. For a refutation of Gregg and Groh's theory, especially regarding their description of Athanasian soteriology as substantialist, see Anatolios, *Coherence of His Thought*, 168–77. In summary of Gregg and Groh's thesis, Anatolios (ibid., 168) writes: "The result is a highly speculative and probably erroneous version of the Arian position and a demonstrably distorted view of the Athanasian position."

Anatolios, Antony is the great model for this Athanasian account of salvation and grace:

> Thus Antony's spirituality, as presented by Athanasius, is not one where divine aid precludes human effort but rather one in which divine aid is seen to be an inducement to greater human effort, with the confidence that comes from trusting that this effort is guaranteed success through the victory of the Incarnate Word.[45]

The Reputation and Character of Athanasius

An account of the contemporary reception of Athanasius would be incomplete without a brief summary of the intense dispute over his character and reputation. As we saw in the case of Isaac Newton and John Henry Newman, how one evaluates Athanasius's *teaching* tends to line up with how one views his *character*. This tendency to align theological and moral evaluations of Athanasius continues in the contemporary period, though some scholars, aware of this alignment, consciously resist equating an evaluation of Athanasius's doctrine with an estimation of his moral character.

Athanasius seems to provoke both strong admiration and fierce dislike in equal measure; people tend either to rally to his defense or to go on the warpath against him. In the early modern period, Isaac Newton and William Whiston represent the tendency to discredit Athanasius and to overturn what they perceive as the false aura of holiness and sanctity that surrounds him. This public discrediting of Athanasius gained new momentum in the late nineteenth and early twentieth centuries and has continued to this day. Duane Arnold helpfully catalogues the pro and contra Athanasius writers of this period.[46] We will examine the moral critique of Athanasius through one of his most outspoken recent critics, Timothy Barnes.

Writing not as a theologian but as a historian, Barnes seeks to set the historical record straight concerning the episcopal behavior of Athanasius. In the opening line of the preface to his study of Athanasius and Constantius, Barnes unveils the goal of the work: "The central purpose of this study is to use modern techniques of historical research to probe behind Athanasius' misrepresentations, many of which have held sway for sixteen centuries."[47] It becomes plain that Barnes is not

45. Anatolios, *Coherence of His Thought*, 185.
46. Arnold, *Early Episcopal Career*, 11–23.
47. Barnes, *Athanasius and Constantius*, ix. Barnes indicates his unfavorable orientation to Athanasius

approaching the historical evidence as a neutral observer; he comes with the force of a prosecuting attorney to make his case against Athanasius and overturn what he believes to be long-held misrepresentations. He presumes from the start that Athanasius's own testimony is tainted and cannot be trusted: "This study starts from the presumption that Athanasius consistently misrepresented central facts about his ecclesiastical career, in particular about his relationship with the emperor Constantine and his three sons . . . and about his own standing within the Christian church in the eastern half of the empire."[48] For Barnes, the very fact that Athanasius was heralded in his own day as an impressive figure provides damning evidence against his presumed humility: "He could not have cut such an impressive figure had he not been conspicuously lacking in the Christian virtues of meekness and humility."[49]

Barnes rehearses in detail the charges of misbehavior leveled against Athanasius and concludes that "Athanasius exercised power and protected his position in Alexandria by the systematic use of violence and intimidation."[50] Further, "Athanasius' primary techniques in the *History of the Arians* are suppression and distortion. . . . The omissions are matched by tendentious misrepresentations. . . . As a result, the *History of the Arians* is a systematically deceptive work."[51] This characterization matches Barnes's earlier estimation of Athanasius's moral character: "Like a modern gangster, he evoked widespread mistrust, proclaimed total innocence—and usually succeeded in evading conviction of specific charges."[52] Barnes accounts for Athanasius's popularity and his ability to persuade so many of the rightness of his cause by pointing to Athanasius's skill as a liar and deceiver. He was not only a bad man but also clever in convincing others that he was not.[53]

A second line of contemporary scholarship acknowledges deep flaws in Athanasius's character but is more moderate in estimation. Richard Hanson makes reference to "the darker side" of Athanasius's character and, accepting the case made by Barnes at least in part, judges that he is at points guilty of "equivocation, not to say mendacity," and that he behaved "like an employer of thugs hired to intimidate his enemies."[54]

by selecting a dedicatory quotation from William Whiston, an avowed Arian from the eighteenth century who published a work attacking Athanasius's character.

48. Ibid., 2.
49. Ibid., 1.
50. Ibid., 33.
51. Ibid., 128–29.
52. Timothy D. Barnes, *Constantine and Eusebius* (Cambridge, MA: Harvard University Press, 1981), 230.
53. Barnes, *Athanasius and Constantius*, 3, 33.

Yet, Hanson acknowledges more virtuous aspects to Athanasius's character: "That he had courage nobody could possibly deny. . . . And as far as tenacity of purpose goes, his career speaks for itself. He was not lastingly vindictive. . . . By the time he died he had been reconciled to almost all of his early enemies."[55] Frances Young attempts to maintain a balance between the "good tradition" surrounding the figure of Athanasius and the "revisionist picture" presented by Barnes and others in the late twentieth century.[56] She allows that "there seems to have been a pitiless streak in his character" but cautions against going too far in blackening his character: "This 'deflation' of Athanasius may go too far; some elements in the good tradition are certainly right."[57]

A third contemporary "reading" of Athanasius, while admitting shortcomings, leans toward the positive view of his character. Surprisingly, Adolph von Harnack, though a strong critic of Athanasius's theology, provides a glowing estimation of his character: "In the midst of this Athanasius alone in the East stood like a rock in the sea. If we measure him by the standards of his time we can discover nothing ignoble or mean about him. The favorite charge of hierarchical imperiousness has something naïve about it."[58]

Duane Arnold has written the most thorough study to date of the early career of Athanasius, complete with a comprehensive review and evaluation of the charges against him. Sifting the evidence from Athanasius's day and other sources that have come to light more recently, Arnold cautiously concludes that Athanasius's critics, ancient and contemporary, have not made a compelling case against him:

> To assert an absolute or certain historical knowledge concerning the character of Athanasius is, of course, difficult, if not impossible. It is possible, however, to arrive at certain reasonable conclusions on the basis of a critical examination of the documentary evidence at hand in order to assess the probability of the truthfulness of the accounts contained within such materials. . . . If this rigorous standard of judgment is applied, it must be admitted that the more vituperative critics of Athanasius have failed to provide clear and convincing evidence for a revisionist portrait of the bishop of Alexandria.[59]

54. Hanson, *Search for the Christian Doctrine*, 243–44, 254.
55. Ibid., 241–42.
56. Young, *From Nicaea to Chalcedon*, 49–50.
57. Ibid., 51.
58. Harnack, *History of Dogma*, 62.
59. Arnold, *Early Episcopal Career*, 98–99.

Arnold judges the two extreme positions on Athanasius to be uncritical: one is too accepting, the other too partisan. He admits that Athanasius "is not at first sight a wholly attractive personality. Intrigue seems to have surrounded him from the earliest days of his episcopate. . . . He shared many of the aggressive qualities of his age."[60] He further proposes that "the application of modern standards of conduct upon fourth-century personalities is sometimes less helpful in any enquiry of this sort."[61] Nevertheless, he arrives at the conclusion that

> there is far less evidence for the violent and duplicitous character of Athanasius than might be supposed from a cursory reading of Hanson, Barnes, or the other current critics. . . . If the many accusations against Athanasius during the early years of his episcopate cannot be dismissed out of hand, they must at least be considered unproved.[62]

Khaled Anatolios follows Arnold in sounding a cautionary note on the ability of historical research to make firm judgments on past controversies: "We also have to concede that the application of historiography to rendering moral judgments of personal character is a complex and perilous matter, especially if it ignores the historicity and variability of norms of conduct in different cultures and different times."[63] He concludes, however, with a positive appreciation of Athanasius's character: "Above all, a judicious evaluation of Athanasius's character must give due weight to the undeniable fact, conceded even by his most vehement of his modern critics, that he eventually gained the overwhelming support and admiration of his own people."[64]

Conclusion

Athanasius possesses a rich legacy in the Christian tradition. But from first to last this legacy has been contested. In his own lifetime, a fierce battle was fought over his fitness for episcopal office and the adequacy of his teaching on the Son of God, with allies and opponents outspoken on either side. With the triumph of Nicene orthodoxy, Athanasius became an iconic figure who stood for the truth against all odds and preserved the biblical doctrine of the full divinity of the Son. Gregory of Nazianzen's panegyric to Athanasius superbly captures this deep

60. Ibid., 175–76.
61. Ibid., 176.
62. Ibid., 183, 186.
63. Anatolios, *Athanasius*, 34.
64. Ibid., 35.

appreciation for both the teaching and character of the great Alexandrian bishop. This view of Athanasius is the dominant picture that remains in the churches of the East and West today.

The story of the reception of Athanasius is one in which a selection of his teaching is appropriated and applied to new questions. In the East, a generous portion of his writings was readily available; he was revered, respected, and often cited, even though his theology, per se, does not appear to have played a primary, foundational role in the formation of Byzantine thought. In the West, a narrower portion of his genuine works was available; ironically, he was best known for a work that he did not compose, the Athanasian Creed. In the early modern period, as his writings became more readily available in the West, a new appropriation of his thought occurred, but critics of both his theology and his character reemerged. This critical scouring of the career and writings of Athanasius has marked the contemporary era and renewed the debate over his theological and personal legacy. As he was in his own time, he remains today a sharply contested figure.

Whatever one may conclude about the charges levelled against his episcopal conduct, the theological legacy of Athanasius remains impressive. In the words of John Behr, "this shadow side to the legendary figure does not do much to reduce his significance for Christian history and theology: Nicene Christianity exists by virtue of his constancy and vision."[65] Khaled Anatolios expands on the significance of Athanasius for the Christian tradition:

> What is of enduring significance for the Christian tradition, however, is not ultimately so much the personality of Athanasius—which cannot be wholly reconstructed with any objective certainty—as his central conviction that genuine Christianity stands or falls by the confession of the full divinity of the Word. It is as a theologian who gave consistent and tireless expression to this claim of faith, and not as a paragon of meekness, mildness, and politesse in debate (conceived according to modern standards!), that Athanasius continues to be a towering figure among the pioneering architects of the Christian tradition.[66]

What I find most striking is that Athanasius consistently landed, often as a pioneer, on the "orthodox" side of many important questions and issues. It was Athanasius who in the later part of his career untiringly explained the significance of Nicaea's confession that the Son is

65. Behr, *Nicene Faith*, part 1, 167.
66. Anatolios, *Athanasius*, 39.

homoousion with the Father and helped to forge an alliance that eventually resulted in the pro-Nicene consensus. It was Athanasius who offered a first draft of a defense of the divinity of the Holy Spirit, showing not only that the Spirit is fully God but also that through the Spirit human beings can attain holiness and deification. It was Athanasius who, late in life, offered an account of the person of Christ, how the single person of the Word was through the incarnation both divine and human at once. And it was Athanasius who, through the *Life of Antony* and his own alliance with the Egyptian desert, shaped an ascetical theology for both East and West and set a pattern for cooperative partnership between the desert and the city. Even when we take into account the limitations, omissions, and inadequacies of Athanasius's thought, this legacy amounts to a remarkable accomplishment, aptly summed up by Frances Young:

> He was to become known as the "Father of Orthodoxy," and deserved this title not merely because of his stubborn resistance to every attack upon his person and the principles for which he stood, but also because of his careful closeness to the nuances of theological development so that the orthodox tradition owes an enormous debt to his theological writings. In the later theological controversies, he will be the one all sides seek to own; and he alone of the Eastern Fathers had an immediate, direct, and lasting influence in the West.[67]

67. Young, *From Nicaea to Chalcedon*, 71.

Bibliography

Primary Texts

Athanasius of Alexandria. *The Letters of Saint Athanasius Concerning the Holy Spirit*. Translated by C. R. B. Shapland. New York: Philosophical Library, 1951.

_____. *St. Athanasius: Select Works and Letters. Nicene and Post-Nicene Fathers*, series 2, vol. 4. Translated by Philip Schaff and Henry Wace. Edinburgh: T&T Clark, 1986.

Basil of Caesarea. *St. Basil: Letters and Select Works. Nicene and Post-Nicene Fathers*, series 2, vol. 8. Translated by Philip Schaff and Henry Wace. Edinburgh: T&T Clark, 1986.

Cyril of Alexandria. *Commentary on John*. 2 vols. Translated by David R. Maxwell. Edited by Joel C. Elowsky. Ancient Christian Texts. Downers Grove, IL: InterVarsity Press, 2013–15.

_____. *Festal Letters 1–12*. Translated by Philip R. Amidon. Edited by John J. O'Keefe. Fathers of the Church 118. Washington, DC: Catholic University of America Press: 2009.

_____. *Letter to the Monks of Egypt*. Translated by John McGuckin. In *St. Cyril of Alexandria and the Christological Controversy*, by John McGuckin, 245–61. Crestwood, NY: St. Vladimir's Seminary Press, 2004.

_____. *Three Christological Treatises*. Translated by Daniel King. Fathers of the Church 129. Washington, DC: Catholic University of America Press, 2014.

Gregory of Nazianzus. *S. Cyril of Jerusalem, S. Gregory of Nazianzus*. Nicene and Post-Nicene Fathers, series 2, vol. 7. Translated by Philip Schaff and Henry Wace. Edinburgh: T&T Clark, 1986.

Jerome. *Theodoret, Jerome, Gennadius, Rufinus*. Nicene and Post-Nicene Fathers, series 2, vol. 3. Translated by Philip Schaff and Henry Wace. Edinburgh: T&T Clark, 1986.

John of Damascus. *On the Divine Images: Three Apologies Against Those Who Attack the Divine Images*. Translated by David Anderson. Crestwood, NY: St. Vladimir's Seminary Press, 1980.

_____. *St. John of Damascus: Writings*. Translated by Frederic H. Chase. Fathers of the Church 37. Washington, DC: Catholic University of America Press, 1958.

Leo the Great. *St. Leo the Great: Letters*. Translated by Edmund Hunt. Fathers of the Church 34. Washington, DC: Catholic University of America Press, 1957.

Newman, John Henry. *Apologia Pro Vita Sua*. Garden City, NY: Doubleday, 1956.

_____. *The Arians of the Fourth Century*. 3rd ed. London: E. Lumley, 1871.

_____. *Certain Difficulties Felt by Anglicans in Catholic Teaching*. Vol. 1. New York: Longmans, Green, 1908.

_____. *An Essay on the Development of Christian Doctrine*. Edited by Charles F. Harrold. New York: Longmans, Green, 1949.

_____. *Lectures on Justification*. 6th ed. London: Longmans, Green, 1892.

_____. *Parochial and Plain Sermons*. San Francisco: Ignatius Press, 1987.

_____. *Select Treatises of St. Athanasius in Controversy with the Arians*. 2 vols. London: Longmans, Green, 1903.

Theodore the Studite. *On the Holy Icons*. Translated by Catharine P. Roth. Crestwood, NY: St. Vladimir's Seminary Press, 2001.

Thomas Aquinas. *The "Summa Theologica" of St. Thomas Aquinas*. Part 1. Translated by the Fathers of the Dominican Province. 2nd rev. ed. 10 vols. London: Burns, Oates & Washbourne, 1920–22. http://tinyurl.com/lco8ktd.

Secondary Texts

Ackroyd, Peter. *Newton*. London: Chatto & Windus, 2006.

Anatolios, Khaled. *Athanasius*. London: Routledge, 2004.

_____. *Athanasius: The Coherence of His Thought*. London: Routledge, 1998.

Arnold, Duane Wade-Hampton. *The Early Episcopal Career of Athanasius of Alexandria*. Notre Dame: University of Notre Dame Press, 1991.

Ayers, Lewis. *Nicaea and Its Legacy: An Approach to Fourth-Century Trinitarian Theology*. Oxford: Oxford University Press, 2004.

Barnes, Michel René. "De Régnon Reconsidered." *Augustinian Studies* 26, no. 2 (1995): 51–79.

_____. "The Fourth Century as Trinitarian Canon." In *Christian Origins: Theology, Rhetoric, and Community*, edited by Lewis Ayres and Gareth Jones, 47–67. London: Routledge, 1998.

Barnes, Timothy D. *Athanasius and Constantius: Theology and Politics in the Constantinian Empire*. Cambridge, MA: Harvard University Press, 1993.

_____. *Constantine and Eusebius*. Cambridge, MA: Harvard University Press, 1981.

Beeley, Christopher A. "Cyril of Alexandria and Gregory Nazianzen: Tradition and Complexity in Patristic Christology." *Journal of Early Christian Studies* 17, no. 3 (2009): 381–419.

_____. *Gregory of Nazianzus on the Trinity and the Knowledge of God: In Your Light We Shall See Light*. New York: Oxford University Press, 2008.

_____. *The Unity of Christ: Continuity and Conflict in Patristic Tradition*. New Haven: Yale University Press, 2012.

Behr, John. *Formation of Christian Faith*. Vol. 2, *The Nicene Faith*, 2 parts. Crestwood, NY: St. Vladimir's Seminary Press, 2004.

Boulnois, Marie-Odile. *Le paradoxe trinitaire chez Cyrille d'Alexandrie*. Paris: Institut des Études Augustiniennes, 1994.

Brakke, David. *Athanasius and the Politics of Asceticism*. Oxford: Clarendon, 1995.

Bray, Gerald. "Whosoever Will Be Saved: The Athanasian Creed and the Modern Church." In *Evangelicals and Nicene Faith: Reclaiming the Apostolic Witness*, edited by Timothy George, 45–57. Grand Rapids: Baker Academic, 2011.

Campbell, Theodore C. "The Doctrine of the Holy Spirit in the Theology of Athanasius." *Scottish Journal of Theology* 27, no. 4 (1974): 408–40.

Chadwick, Henry. *East and West: The Making of a Rift in the Church: From Apostolic Times until the Council of Florence*. Oxford: Oxford University Press, 2003.

Cross, Frank L. *The Study of St. Athanasius*. Oxford: Clarendon, 1945.

Daley, Brian E. "The Fullness of the Saving God: Cyril of Alexandria on the Holy Spirit." In *The Theology of Cyril of Alexandria: A Critical Appreciation*, edited by Thomas G. Weinandy and Daniel A. Keating, 113–48. London: T&T Clark, 2003.

Denzinger, Heinrich, comp. *Compendium of Creeds, Definitions, and Declarations on Matters of Faith and Morals*. 43rd ed. San Francisco: Ignatius Press, 2012.

Dragas, George Dion. *St. Athanasius of Alexandria: Original Research and New Perspectives*. Rollinsford, NH: Orthodox Research Institute, 2005.

Drobner, Hubertus R. *The Fathers of the Church: A Comprehensive Introduction*. Translated by Siegfried S. Schatzmann. Peabody, MA: Hendrickson, 2007.

Dry, Sarah. *The Newton Papers: The Strange and True Odyssey of Isaac Newton's Manuscripts*. Oxford: Oxford University Press, 2014.

Ernest, James D. *The Bible in Athanasius*. Leiden: Brill, 2004.

Gemeinhardt, Peter, ed., *Athanasius Handbuch*. Tübingen: Mohr Siebeck, 2011.

Gill, Joseph. *The Council of Florence*. Cambridge: Cambridge University Press, 1959.

Gregg, Robert C., and Dennis E. Groh. *Early Arianism: A View of Salvation*. Philadelphia: Fortress Press, 1981.

Grillmeier, Aloys. *Christ in Christian Tradition*. Vol. 1, *From the Apostolic Age to Chalcedon (451)*. Translated by J. S. Bowden. London: Mowbray, 1965.

Gwynn, David M. *Athanasius of Alexandria: Bishop, Theologian, Ascetic, Father*. Oxford: Oxford University Press, 2012.

Hanson, R. P. C. *The Search for the Christian Doctrine of God: The Arian Controversy 318–381*. Edinburgh: T&T Clark, 1988.

Harnack, Adolf von. *History of Dogma*. Vol. 4. Translated by Neil Buchanan. New York: Dover, 1961.

Kannengiesser, Charles. "The Athanasian Decade 1974–84: A Bibliographical Report." *Theological Studies* 46, no. 3 (1985): 524–41.

Kelly, J. N. D. *The Athanasian Creed*. London: A&C Black, 1964.

Ker, Ian. *John Henry Newman: A Biography*. Oxford: Clarendon, 1988.

Leithart, Peter J. *Athanasius*. Grand Rapids: Baker Academic, 2011.

Louth, Andrew. "Manhood into God: The Oxford Movement, the Fathers and the Deification of Man." In *Essays Catholic and Radical*, edited by Kenneth Leech and Rowan Williams, 70–80. London: Bowerdean, 1983.

Mamiani, Maurizio. "Newton on Prophecy and the Apocalypse." In *The Cambridge Companion to Newton*, edited by I. Bernard Cohen and George E. Smith, 387–408. Cambridge: Cambridge University Press, 2002.

Mandelbrote, Scott. "Newton and Eighteenth-Century Christianity." In *The Cambridge Companion to Newton*, edited by I. Bernard Cohen and George E. Smith, 409–30. Cambridge: Cambridge University Press, 2002.

Manuel, Frank E. *The Religion of Isaac Newton: The Fremantle Lectures of 1973*. Oxford: Clarendon, 1974.

Mendham, John, trans. *The Seventh General Council, the Second of Nicaea: In Which the Worship of Images Was Established*. London: W. E. Painter, 1849.

Molloy, Michael E. *Champion of Truth: The Life of Saint Athanasius*. New York: Society of St. Paul, 2003.

Pelikan, Jaroslav. *The Christian Tradition*. Vol. 4, *Reformation of Church and Dogma (1300–1700)*. Chicago: University of Chicago Press, 1984.

Pettersen, Alvyn. *Athanasius*. Ridgefield, CT: Morehouse, 1995.

Robertson, Jon M. *Christ as Mediator: A Study of the Theologies of Eusebius of Caesarea, Marcellus of Ancyra, and Athanasius of Alexandria*. Oxford: Oxford University Press, 2007.

Russell, Norman. *Cyril of Alexandria*. London: Routledge, 2000.

_____. *The Doctrine of Deification in the Greek Patristic Tradition*. Oxford: Oxford University Press, 2004.

Sparks, Jack N. *The Resurrection Letters*. Nashville: Thomas Nelson, 1979.

Strange, Roderick. "Newman and the Mystery of Christ." In *Newman After a Hun-*

dred Years, edited by Ian Kerr and Alan G. Hill, 323–36. Oxford: Clarendon, 1990.

Thomas, Stephen. *Newman and Heresy: The Anglican Years.* Cambridge: Cambridge University Press, 1991.

Weinandy, Thomas G. *Athanasius: A Theological Introduction.* Aldershot, UK: Ashgate, 2007.

_____. *The Father's Spirit of Sonship: Reconceiving the Trinity.* Edinburgh: T&T Clark, 1995.

Westfall, Richard S. *The Life of Isaac Newton.* Cambridge: Cambridge University Press, 1993.

White, Michael. *Isaac Newton: The Last Sorcerer.* Reading, MA: Addison-Wesley, 1997.

Wickham, Lionel. Introduction to *Cyril of Alexandria: Select Letters*, edited and translated by Lionel Wickham, xi–xlix. Oxford: Clarendon, 1983.

Wiles, Maurice. *Archetypal Heresy: Arianism through the Centuries.* New York: Oxford University Press, 1996.

Wilken, Robert. "Introducing the Athanasian Creed." *Currents in Theology and Mission* 6, no. 1 (1979): 4–10.

Williams, Rowan. *Arius: Heresy and Tradition.* Rev. ed. Grand Rapids: Eerdmans, 2001.

_____. "Newman's *Arians* and the Question of Method in Doctrinal History." In *Newman after a Hundred Years*, edited by Ian Kerr and Alan G. Hill, 263–85. Oxford: Clarendon, 1990.

Young, Frances M. *From Nicaea to Chalcedon: A Guide to the Literature and Background.* With Andrew Teal. 2nd ed. Grand Rapids: Baker Academic, 2010.

Index of Names

Aetius, 52
Alexander of Alexandria, 1
Ambrose of Milan, 81
Anatolios, Khaled, 7n1, 64, 64n32, 111, 111n23, 115–16, 115n41, 115n44, 116n45, 119, 119n63, 120, 120n66, 124
Antony of the Desert, 75
Arius, 2–3, 7, 9–17, 21, 41, 55, 89–90, 90n13, 93–95, 99, 99n61, 100, 113, 127
Arnold, Duane Wade-Hampton, 52n4, 83, 83n44, 116, 116n46, 118–19, 118n59, 124
Augustine of Hippo, 28, 74, 81, 103
Ayres, Lewis, 7n1, 56, 56n6, 124

Barnes, Michel René, 80n33, 124
Barnes, Timothy D., 52n4, 116–17, 117n52, 124
Barth, Karl, 99
Basil of Ancyra, 4, 23
Basil of Caesarea, 56, 123
Beeley, Christopher A., 60n18, 64, 64n35, 65, 65nn36–37, 107, 108n7, 110–13, 110n17, 114nn34–35, 125
Behr, John, 7n1, 56, 56n4, 67, 67n49, 111–12, 112n26, 115, 115n41, 120, 120n65, 125
Boulnois, Marie-Odile, 63, 63n29
Brakke, David, 7n1, 66, 66n41, 67, 67n46, 125

Caesarius of Arles, 77, 81–82
Calvin, John, 84, 84n48
Clarke, Samuel, 94–95
Clement of Alexandria, 96
Constans I (emperor), 3
Constantine I (emperor), 2, 12, 117
Constantius II (emperor), 3–4, 116
Cross, Frank L., 67, 67n48, 74, 125
Cyril of Alexandria, xii, 44n14, 46, 56, 60–61, 62nn23–24, 63nn25–27, 63n30, 64n33, 64n35, 65n37, 82, 82n42, 123, 125–27

Daley, Brian E., 63, 63n30, 125
Didymus the Blind, 63
Dionysius, 96
Dragas, George Dion, 7n1, 55, 55n3, 102, 102n74, 125
Dry, Sarah, 88n3, 93n28, 125

Eugenicus, Mark, 71
Eunomius, 52, 94–95

Eusebius of Nicomedia, 2
Eutyches, 76, 99

Froude, Hurrell, 96

George of Alexandria, 4
Gregg, Robert C., 113, 113n31, 115, 115n44, 125
Gregory of Nazianzus, xi, xii, 34n34, 46, 46n24, 56, 58–60, 58nn11–13, 59nn14–17, 60nn18–19, 64–66, 64n35, 66nn39–40, 73, 119, 123, 125
Gregory of Nyssa, 56
Grillmeier, Aloys, 44n14, 109, 109nn11–12, 109n15, 126
Groh, Dennis E., 113, 113n31, 115, 115n44, 125
Gwynn, David, 51, 51n1, 52n2, 55n2, 60n18, 66n38, 67, 67n45, 73, 73n1, 74n3, 75–77, 75nn5–7, 76n16, 77n19, 106n2, 126

Hanson, R. P. C., 61n22, 107, 108n6, 110, 110n16, 112n28, 114, 114n35, 115, 117–19, 118n54, 126
Harnack, Adolph von, 107, 107n5, 114n36, 118, 118n58, 126
Hilary of Poitiers, 74–75

Jerome, 60n20, 74–76, 75nn9–11, 123
John Chrysostom, xi, 73
John of Damascus, 68, 68nn51–52, 69n53, 124
Julian (the Apostate), 76
Julius I (pope), 3

Keble, John, 96, 102n72
Kelly, J. N. D., 77, 77n18, 77n21, 77n23, 78n24, 79n28, 80, 80n31, 80n34, 81, 81nn37–39, 82n40, 114n36, 126
Ker, Ian, 87n2, 95n44, 97n52, 101n67, 102, 102n73, 102n75, 126, 127

Leithart, Peter J., 112n28, 126
Leo the Great (pope), 74, 76, 76n17, 124
Liberius (pope), 4
Locke, John, 93, 93n33
Luther, Martin, 84

Mandelbrote, Scott, 89n9, 91n23, 92n25, 93n33, 126
Manuel, Frank E., 90n13, 91n19, 93n29, 95n41, 126
Marcellus of Ancyra, 82n41, 107, 126
Mary (the virgin), 38, 42
Maximus the Confessor, 70
Melanchthon, Philip, 84
Melitius of Antioch, 57
Melitius of Lycopolis, 2
Montenero, John, 71

Nestorius, 46, 64, 76, 99
Newman, John Henry, xii, 11n2, 53, 87, 87n2, 88, 95–97, 95nn43–44, 96n45, 96nn47–48, 97n52, 97nn54–55, 98–103, 98n57, 98n59, 99n60, 100n64, 100n66, 101nn67–70, 102nn71–73, 102n75, 103n78, 116, 124, 126–27
Newton, Isaac, xii, 53, 87–95, 87n1, 88nn3–5, 89nn6–11, 90nn12–14, 90n16, 91nn18–24, 92nn25–27, 93nn28–29, 93n33, 95n41, 103, 107, 116, 124–27

O'Keefe, John J., 62n23, 63, 64n31, 123
Origen of Alexandria, 8–9, 22, 96

Paulinus, 57
Pettersen, Alvyn, 7n1, 112, 112n29, 114, 115n39, 126
Philostorgius, 52, 52n4
Pius V (pope), 73, 79

Russell, Norman, 63–64, 63n26, 64nn33–34, 68n50, 114, 114n36, 126

Serapion of Thmuis, 29
Socrates (church historian), 52, 52n2, 68
Sozomen, 52, 68
Sparks, Jack N., 61n21, 126

Theodore the Studite, 69, 69n55, 124
Theodoret, 52, 52n2, 68, 75n11, 123
Theophilus of Alexandria, 66
Thomas Aquinas, 28n9, 70, 70n57, 74, 74n4, 78, 78n26, 124
Thomas, Stephen, 97, 97n54, 101n70, 127

Valens (emperor), 5, 75
Valentinian I (emperor), 5
Vincent of Lérins, 81

Weinandy, Thomas G., xi, 7n1, 31n21, 63n30, 108, 108nn9–10, 111n23, 115, 115n40, 125, 127
Westfall, Richard S., 87n1, 88, 88n4, 89n7, 89n10, 90, 90n12, 90n16, 91n22, 91n24, 92n27, 93n33, 127
Whiston, William, 94, 116, 117n47
White, Michael, 88n5, 90, 90n14, 91n18, 92n26, 127
Wickham, Lionel, 63, 63n27, 127
Wiles, Maurice, 84n48, 90n15, 93, 93n30, 93nn33–34, 94n36, 127
Williams, Rowan, 95, 95n44, 96n47, 99, 99n61, 102n72, 126–27

Young, Frances, 7, 52n3, 63n30, 109n15, 118, 118n56, 121, 121n67, 127